Successful Site-Based Management

Successful Site-Based Management

A Practical Guide

Revised Edition

Larry J. Reynolds

CORWIN PRESS, INC.
A Sage Publications Company
Thousand Oaks, California

Copyright © 1997 by Corwin Press, Inc.

All rights reserved. Use of the worksheets in each chapter is authorized for local schools and noncommercial entities only. Except for that usage, no part of this book may be reproduced or utilized in any form or by any means, electronic or mechanical, including photocopying, recording, or by any information storage and retrieval system, without permission in writing from the publisher.

For information address:

Corwin Press, Inc.
A Sage Publications Company
2455 Teller Road
Thousand Oaks, California 91320
e-mail: order@corwin.sagepub.com

SAGE Publications Ltd.
6 Bonhill Street
London EC2A 4PU
United Kingdom

SAGE Publications India Pvt. Ltd.
M-32 Market
Greater Kailash I
New Delhi 110 048 India

Printed in the United States of America

Library of Congress Cataloging-in-Publication Data

Reynolds, Larry J. (Larry Joseph), 1942–
    Successful site-based management : a practical guide / Larry J. Reynolds.
       p. cm.
    Includes bibliographical references.
    ISBN 0-8039-6559-1 (acid-free paper). — ISBN 0-8039-6560-5 (pbk. : acid-free paper)
     1. School-based management—United States. 2. School improvement programs—United States. 3. Educational planning—United States.
I. Title.
LB2806.35.R49   1997
371.2—dc21   96-51301

This book is printed on acid-free paper.

97 98 99 00 01 10 9 8 7 6 5 4 3 2 1

Corwin Press Production Editor: S. Marlene Head
Editorial Assistant: Nicole Fountain
Typesetter: Rebecca Evans
Cover Designer: Marcia R. Finlayson

Contents

List of Figures	ix
List of Tables	x
List of Worksheets	xi
Preface	xiii
About the Author	xvi
1. Introduction to Site-Based Management	**1**
School Improvement and Site-Based Management	2
Site-Based Management Defined	2
But What Does This Really Mean?	3
The Uncertainty of Change	3
Is It Worth the Effort?	4
A Strategy for Implementing Site-Based Management	4
2. New Perspectives, Knowledge, and Skills	**6**
Defining Success	6
Components of Success	7
Adopting a Systemwide Perspective	8
Understanding the Context of Change	9
Developing Leadership Perspectives and Skills	9
Creating a Shared Vision	11
Developing Strategic Planning Skills	12
Defining New Roles	13
The Scenario of "Too Much"	14
The Scenario of "Too Little"	14
Enhancing the Work Environment	15

Understanding Group Dynamics	17
Clarifying Accountability	18
Recommended Steps in Implementing Site-Based Management	19

3. The Role of the Central Office — 23

Adopting a Leadership Perspective	23
Understanding the Context of Change	25
Current Status of Site-Based Management	25
Current Issues and Programs	30

4. Strategic Planning and Site-Based Management — 35

The Strategic Planning Model	36
External Forces	37
Needs of Students (Current and Future)	40
Values, Beliefs, and Expectations	43
The Vision	45
Checking the Vision	48
Next Steps	48

5. Putting the Vision to Work — 49

Setting and Communicating Expectations and Parameters	51
Criteria for Evaluation	52
Steps in Implementing	53
Expected Benefits	53
Types of Budget, Staffing, and Program Decisions	55
Required Districtwide Goals and Programs	57
Identifying the Management Needs of Schools	59
Creating Support Roles for Leadership and Service	61
Accountability	64

6. The Principal: The Key to Success — 66

Adopting a Systemwide Perspective	67
The External System	68
The Internal System	68
Understanding the Context of Change	69
Increasing Organizational Effectiveness	74
Meeting the Management Needs of the School	75
Creating a Positive Organizational Climate	77
Influencing Attitudes and Beliefs About Change	79
Developing a Schoolwide Perspective of the Educational Program	79
Adopting the Strategic Planning Model for School Improvement	80
Summary	81

7. Expanding the Role of the Principal	83
Adopting Leadership Behaviors	84
Establishing Credibility	84
Developing Trust	86
Vision and Inspiration	97
Summary of Leadership Requirements for the Principal	99
Defining New Roles and Accountability	99
8. Structuring the Site Team for Success	103
Getting Started	105
Group Size	106
Group Diversity	109
Criteria for Selecting Members	109
Different Status of Members	110
Group Norms	111
Work Setting	111
Summary	111
Initial Activities	113
Getting to Know Each Other	113
Defining Communication Needs	116
Reviewing and Revising Group Norms	118
Reviewing External Influences on the Team	120
Understanding the Context of Change	120
Selecting Members for Leadership Positions	123
Reviewing the Yearly Cycle	123
Summary	126
9. Learning New Skills	127
Leadership Skills	127
Strategic Planning Skills	130
Problem-Solving and Decision-Making Skills	132
Defining the Problem	133
Identifying the Causes of Problems	135
Brainstorming Possible Solutions	139
Evaluating and Selecting Alternatives	141
Implementing Solutions	141
Summary	144
10. Working With the School Community	145
The Importance of a Shared Vision of the Future	146
Accomplishing the Task	147
Participation	148

  Phase 1: Creating the Shared Vision   149
   Activity 1: Review of the Districtwide Strategic Plan   150
   Activity 2: Generating the Shared Vision   153
   Activity 3: Finalizing the Shared Vision   153
  Phase 2: The Current Program and Priorities for the Future   156
   Activity 1: Identifying Current Program Strengths   157
   Activity 2: Identifying Areas for Future Development   157
   Activity 3: Selecting Current Priorities   158
   Activity 4: Generating Ideas for School Improvement Priorities   159
  Phase 3: Planning and Implementing Program Improvements   162
  Evaluating School Improvement Efforts   163

11. How Do We Know If We Are Making Progress?   166
  The Role of the Districtwide Advisory Group   167
  Monitoring the Process of Implementation   168
  Meeting the Timeline   170
  Monitoring Site-Team Issues and Decisions   172
  Noticing the Small Changes, Big Effects   176
  Questions to Ask During the Early Stages   177
  Questions to Ask After Implementation   179
  Traditional Concerns of the Central Office   179
  Changing Beliefs, Values, and Assumptions   180
  The Promise of Site-Based Management   181

References   183

List of Figures

Figure 2.1. Relationship Between Site-Based Management and Student Success — 7

Figure 2.2. Teacher Hierarchy of Concerns — 16

Figure 4.1. First Four Steps in District-Level Strategic Planning — 37

Figure 5.1. District-Level Strategic Planning Model — 51

Figure 6.1. Goals of Site-Based Management — 75

Figure 6.2. Increasing Organizational Effectiveness — 76

Figure 9.1. School-Level Strategic Planning Model — 132

Figure 11.1. Traditional Concerns of the Central Office — 181

List of Tables

Table 2.1	Differences Between Management and Leadership	10
Table 2.2	Leadership Characteristics	11
Table 2.3	Accountability in Site-Based Management	20
Table 2.4	Steps in Implementing Site-Based Management	21
Table 4.1	Categories of External Forces	38
Table 4.2	Definition of the Three Vision Categories	45
Table 4.3	Sample Vision	46
Table 5.1	New Service Roles of the Central Office	62
Table 6.1	Management Needs of Schools	77
Table 6.2	Organizational Climate Components	79
Table 6.3	Basic Orientations Toward School Change	80
Table 6.4	Steps to Increase School Effectiveness	81
Table 7.1	Steps in Building the Leadership Role of the Principal	85
Table 7.2	Skills and Behaviors Required of the Principal	100
Table 8.1	Strengths and Weaknesses of Group Decision Making	105
Table 11.1	Questions to Ask After Implementation	180

List of Worksheets

1. Reasons for Adopting Site-Based Management	26
2. Deciding on Site-Based Management	27
3. Clarity About New Roles and Responsibilities	28
4. Current Level of Support	29
5. Inventory of Districtwide Issues	31
6. Inventory of Special Programs and Projects	32
7. Inventory of Program and Project Decision Makers	33
8. External Forces: Current and Future	39
9. Students' Current Needs and Implications	41
10. Students' Future Needs and Implications	42
11. Values, Beliefs, and Expectations	44
12. Vision Categories	47
13. Expectations for Site-Based Management	54
14. Expectations Concerning Decision Making	56
15. Required Districtwide Programs	58
16. Central Office Assistance With Management Needs	60
17. Principal's Survey of Major Issues and Problems	70
18. Principal's Inventory of Special Programs and Projects	71
19. Principal's Inventory of School Decision-Making and Advisory Groups	72
20. Principal's Inventory of Activities and Use of Time	73
21. Current Status of Management Needs	87
22. Accessibility Log for the Principal	89

23. Interactions Initiated by the Principal (Sample Form)	91
24. Interactions Initiated by the Principal	93
25. Principal's Self-Assessment of Trust	95
26. Principal's Assessment of Organizational Climate	96
27. Defining the Role of the Site Team	107
28. Defining the Structure and Membership of the Site Team	112
29. Getting to Know Each Other	115
30. Meeting Communication Needs	117
31. Reviewing and Revising Group Norms	119
32. Current Perceptions of the Context of Change	122
33. Yearly Cycle of Activities, Events, and Decisions	125
34. Developing Site-Team Leadership	129
35. Review of the Districtwide Strategic Plan	131
36. Defining the Problem	134
37. Identifying the Causes of Problems	137
38. Summarizing the Causes of Problems	138
39. Brainstorming Possible Solutions	140
40. Evaluating and Selecting Alternatives	142
41. Implementing Solutions	143
42. Review of the Districtwide Strategic Plan (by the School Community)	152
43. The Shared Vision (by the School Community)	154
44. Future Development Ideas (School Community Group Number ___)	161
45. Using the Strategic Planning Model for Continuous Evaluation	165
46. Monitoring the Process of Implementation	169
47. Suggested Timeline for Implementation	171
48. Checklist of Site-Team Issues and Decisions: School A	173
49. Checklist of Decision Making in Different Schools	175
50. Actual Benefits of Site-Based Management	178

Preface

Site-based management has become a popular, but not well understood, strategy intended to improve public education. Many districts and schools initiate site-based management because they assume it will lead to better quality decisions and improved school programs. Frequently, however, school districts have an incomplete understanding of the process required to attain these goals. As a result, a great deal of time and effort is spent by school participants in improper or incomplete implementation of site-based management. The consequence is frustration, disappointment, burnout, and a quick return to previous patterns. Not only is the immediate promise of site-based management lost, but its failure further reduces the confidence of the organization to make other attempts of change in the future.

This is the general pattern I found, working directly with site teams of administrators, teachers, parents, and students and conducting workshops and classes on site-based management. More specifically, in numerous settings where site-based management had been implemented, building site teams spent the majority of their time on the following:

1. Issues related to organizing the site team and trying to define its purpose
2. Issues that were school management or administrative issues rather than instructional issues
3. Generating proposals that were rejected at higher levels in the district

All of this made it doubtful that site-based management would have a significant effect on the instructional program and student success. At the same time, in these same settings, I was impressed with people's commitment to students, desire to improve the educational program and services of the school, and willingness to devote extra time to do it.

Yet in other settings, although fewer in number, site-based management was characterized by efficient team meetings, a focus on students and the instructional program, decisions about significant changes in the school, studying future changes, and reviewing and evaluating those that had already been made. Even in these settings, however, the loss of key persons led to a loss in the efficiency and effectiveness of the site team. Furthermore, these schools were isolated examples of success in districts where other schools were still struggling with site-based management. The success in these settings, however, demonstrated that site-based management could be an effective decision-making structure for schools.

Another common theme in my interactions and discussions around site-based management was the need of people in the schools, at all levels of the organization, for practical, concrete information on how to make site-based management work. Most of the articles and research known to them was considered too general to be of assistance. The personal experiences of other teachers, parents, and administrators in site-based management schools were helpful, but too many differences existed between districts, schools, and circumstances to copy what had been done elsewhere.

A need, therefore, existed to find an effective way to take what research and theory had to say about such areas as effective leadership and group decision making and identify ways to avoid the problems usually associated with site-based management. My intention was to create a book that would serve as "a guide to action" that could be used in a variety of settings. Furthermore, the guide would need to allow individuals to recognize how the history, needs, and uniqueness of their own setting would influence what was required to implement site-based management effectively.

To this end, this book does the following:

- Provides a systemwide approach to site-based management
- Uses site-based management as a strategy for school improvement and increased student success rather than the management of the status quo
- Identifies nine essential perspectives and skills required to support site-based management
- Defines the new roles and responsibilities of central office personnel, principals, and site teams
- Recommends a specific "how-to" approach of 25 steps to implement site-based management
- Provides worksheets and guidelines to apply to different specific settings

Preface

The intended audience of this book includes school board members, central office administrators, principals, and site-team members. It is hoped the discussions and guidelines in this book will provide people new ways to look at site-based management, help them identify and prepare for the changes it entails, and assist them in applying their knowledge of their own settings to school improvement efforts. In this manner, the book should be helpful to university faculty, district professional development personnel, and educational consultants as well.

The assistance of several people has been instrumental in the preparation of this book. The suggestions and reviews by Betsy Bralts, Bob DeBlauw, Barbara Elvecrog, Bob Everhart, Jerry Mansergh, Neil Nickerson, and Jim Reynolds of early drafts were most helpful. The assistance of Jerry Mansergh and the staff of the Educational Cooperative Service Unit of the Metropolitan Twin Cities Area is deeply appreciated. I would also like to thank all the people I worked with in schools and workshops who so willingly spent time sharing their knowledge and experience about site-based management.

I am especially grateful to A. B. Reynolds for her encouragement, support, and contributions at all stages of this work.

LARRY J. REYNOLDS

About the Author

Larry J. Reynolds is currently an independent consultant in Minneapolis, Minnesota, and has more than 25 years of experience in education as a teacher, principal, college professor, consultant, and director of research and evaluation studies. He has worked in a variety of settings, including research and development centers, regional educational laboratories, public and private schools, universities, and consulting companies. His interests include leadership, organizational development, and educational reform. This is the second edition of his book on site-based management.

1

Introduction to Site-Based Management

There are forces of change acting on our schools today that are simply too strong for "business as usual" to continue. The changing characteristics of our society and communities are causing changes in the students we serve, their needs, and the educational programs and services we must provide. And the future world of work for these students will demand different knowledge and skills than we have focused on in the past. Although these are not new thoughts, the pressure of these forces has intensified to the point that many schools are in a crisis.[1]

Although it is generally agreed that changes are needed, *what* is needed is less clear. More of the same, however, does not appear to be a viable alternative. The need is not increasing the efficiency or effectiveness of current policies, procedures, and programs. The need is to change significantly what we are doing and how we do it. As a result, restructuring schools will be the theme for change in the near future.

Restructuring schools requires that we make major changes in the following areas:

- How we view students and learning
- How we define the programs and services to offer
- How we organize and deliver programs and services
- How we manage our schools

The focus of this book is on how to go about restructuring the management of our schools.

School Improvement and Site-Based Management

Site-based management of schools has emerged as a promising component of school restructuring efforts in American education. Its central theme is easy to grasp—many of the decisions typically made at the central office level will now be made at the individual school level. Advocates of site-based management frequently cite the following advantages:

- The quality of decisions about educational programs will improve if the decisions are made by the persons with the greatest knowledge about a school and its students.
- Change is constant and requires that individual schools are increasingly flexible and responsive.
- Change mandated from the top does not work.
- Participation in decision making will result in higher levels of commitment, effort, and morale.[2]

Because of these reasons, site-based management offers the potential to increase the quality of decisions we make about the other areas key to restructuring efforts: how students and learning are viewed, how the programs and services that are offered are defined, and how programs and services are organized and delivered.

Site-Based Management Defined

Site-based management has been defined by different people in slightly different ways. For our purposes, however, site-based management is defined by three essential components.

1. The delegation of the authority to individual schools to make decisions about the educational program of the school including staffing, budget, and program
2. The adoption of a shared decision-making model at the school level by a management team including the principal, teachers, parents, and sometimes students and other community members
3. An expectation that site-based management will facilitate leadership at the school level in school improvement efforts

But What Does This Really Mean?

Although the idea of individual schools making more decisions sounds like a good one and the advantages are attractive, thinking about site-based management begins to raise all kinds of questions.

1. How does site-based management really work?
2. Who will make what kinds of decisions?
3. How will this change the role of the central office?
4. How will this change what principals do?
5. What new demands will this place on teachers?
6. Will I gain (or lose) power and influence?
7. How does this fit in with all the other stuff we are trying to do?
8. When will we find the time to do this?
9. Is this just another fad we have to endure until it goes away?
10. What does this have to do with student achievement anyway?

The Uncertainty of Change

As the above questions suggest, site-based management may not be such a simple idea after all. Although it calls for significant change in how our schools are run and in who plays what role in decision making, it is not readily apparent what this means at an operational level for different people and for the organization as a whole.

Consequently, even though implementing site-based management is intended to increase the quality of a school's instructional program, its immediate effect is to disrupt the established routine of the school district and individual schools. During this period of disruption, new situations will be encountered and experience will be less relevant as a guide to behavior. Individuals will be challenged to alter their belief systems, acquire new knowledge, develop new skills, and change customary patterns of behavior.

This early disruptive period of change presents the greatest challenge to the successful implementation of site-based management. If not managed well, the problems faced during this period may be so great that site-based management may be discontinued before it has really begun, exist more as a program of words than actions, or be distorted to fit previous patterns of behavior.[3]

However, with all changes there is an initial period of disruption that can be reduced by careful planning. Site-based management does have the potential to be an effective strategy to improve our schools. The purpose of this book is to help schools and school districts to achieve that potential.

Is It Worth the Effort?

Yes. As stated earlier, site-based management can be an effective means of school improvement. But improvement for whom? We believe site-based management, as defined and discussed in this book, can lead to school improvement in two interdependent areas:

1. Educational programs and services for students, parents, and the community
2. Quality of the work environment for all members of the organization

A Strategy for Implementing Site-Based Management

This book will provide a "guide to action" for those schools and districts who are striving for school improvement. Site-based management is presented as a comprehensive strategy to stimulate and organize those school improvement efforts. As a first step, it is necessary to examine further the elements of site-based management and the knowledge, skills, and perspectives necessary to make it a success in any school district. This general discussion is presented in Chapter 2.

The subsequent discussions (and chapters) are keyed to helping the reader examine the various stages of implementing site-based management and apply them to his or her own particular setting. This book is intended to be a practical guide including information about site-based management, suggestions for action, and worksheets to be used by participants at all levels in the school district. Although the overall strategy will be the same for all districts and schools, questions and activities are included that are designed to help identify the particular issues, circumstances, and needs that will influence and affect your own efforts in site-based management.[4]

Notes

1. The literature on school reform is extensive. Fiske (1991) and Smith (1995) provide a school-centered focus on school reform and recommend specific approaches and programs considered successful in increasing student success.

2. Advocates of site-based management have claimed additional benefits as well. A thorough and informative review is provided by Murphy and Beck (1995).

3. The extensive research on the problems encountered while implementing site-based management is reviewed and discussed by Murphy and Beck (1995).

4. A different approach to site-based management that may be helpful to the reader is presented by Glickman (1993).

2

New Perspectives, Knowledge, and Skills

Delegation of authority is fundamental to site-based management. However, merely delegating decisions to another group does not necessarily guarantee an increase in the quality of decisions. And decision making typically takes more time by a group than when done by an individual. If site-based management is to succeed as a more effective decision-making strategy for the organization, then it will have to be supported by accompanying changes in other aspects of the organization as well. This chapter will focus on key components of the organization that must be in place for site-based management to succeed.

Defining Success

How is success defined for site-based management? Site-based management will ultimately be judged in terms of its effect on students. But because site-based management is a decision-making strategy, not an instructional program or a learning strategy, the effect is not direct.

Also, when the positive effect on students is mentioned, it should be clearly defined. Many people believe that if site-based management does not affect student achievement, it is not worth the trouble. However, it is hoped that schools are reaching the point where the success of educational programs is not determined only by standardized measures of student achievement. The broader concept of student success includes a greater variety of ways to measure the effectiveness of our efforts. These might include the following:

New Perspectives, Knowledge, and Skills

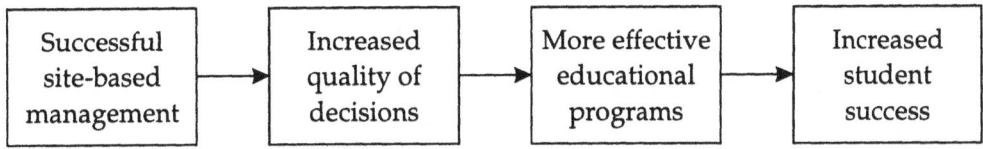

Figure 2.1. Relationship Between Site-Based Management and Student Success

- Higher-order thinking skills
- Multicultural understanding and appreciation
- Dropout rates
- Community service
- Access to electives
- Participation in upper-level math and science classes
- Postsecondary choices and success
- Student self-concept
- Creativity and excellence in the arts

Whatever criteria are selected for student success, its attainment is dependent on the quality of the educational programs and services provided.

The primary focus in this book is how to improve the quality of our decision-making process as educational programs are continued or changed to meet the needs of our students. Therefore, the success of site-based management is defined by the quality of decisions made about educational programs. The relationship between site-based management and student success is shown in Figure 2.1.

Components of Success

As stated earlier, change frequently requires that individuals adopt new belief systems, acquire new knowledge and skills, and alter customary patterns of behavior. This is particularly true for the success of site-based management. There are nine key components that schools must address to support the successful implementation of site-based management.

1. Adopting a systemwide perspective
2. Understanding the context of change

3. Developing leadership perspectives and skills
4. Creating a shared vision
5. Developing strategic planning skills
6. Defining new roles
7. Enhancing the work environment
8. Understanding group dynamics
9. Clarifying accountability

Each of the key components for the successful implementation of site-based management is introduced in this chapter to provide an organization-wide perspective. These nine components are discussed in greater detail throughout the rest of the book.

Adopting a Systemwide Perspective

"Not understanding the big picture" is a flaw usually attributed to others, especially when they fail to understand or appreciate our own position, demands, and limitations. Central office staff often think building personnel fail to realize the districtwide demands, pressures, constraints, and regulations that central office personnel must satisfy. Building personnel often think central office personnel do not understand the effect of their requests and decisions on the people "on the front lines." Principals and teachers often have different ideas about where money and time and energy should be spent. Our perceptions and actions are usually a function of our own needs and priorities. Our ability to understand and respond to the needs and priorities of others is difficult.

Site-based management, however, requires that central office staff, principals, and site-team members have a "big picture" focus. Each must understand the needs, demands, and effect of site-based management on the others. A mutually understood definition of expectations, roles, and accountability must also exist. Site-based management requires a collaborative effort of people at all levels working toward common goals.

The real test of the organization's ability to create a common big picture of site-based management is to ask each participant to accurately describe the role and function of the other participants in making site-based management work in the district and in individual schools.

To this end, it is recommended that all participants of site-based management read all the chapters of this book; that is, site-team members need to understand the issues raised in the chapters on the central office as much as central office members need to be familiar with site-team development issues. Furthermore, although leadership and strategic planning perspectives and skills will be needed by all participants, each needs to know how these are similar and different for different organizational members and groups.

Understanding the Context of Change

The change to site-based management will occur in contexts that vary from district to district and from school to school. As the change is made from one decision-making structure to another, we need to assess carefully where we are now. What is going on? Or, as was asked in the first chapter, "How does site-based management fit into all the other stuff we are trying to do?" This review is so critical that it is the first step in the implementation process.

Site-based management will be influenced by most of the ongoing issues, challenges, and programs of the district. These potentially include

- Externally funded special projects
- Activities related to evaluations required by accreditation agencies
- Cooperative programs with other districts
- Business partnerships
- Future bond issue and tax levy referendums
- New programs mandated at the state level
- Changes in student enrollment
- Future retirements of district and building personnel

These will all affect how site-based management will function and the issues it must address. Furthermore, these ongoing programs and issues will compete with each other and with site-based management for the attention, time, and energy of both district and building personnel. The potential of site-based management, however, is to coordinate and bring order to these multiple demands.

Developing Leadership Perspectives and Skills

Leadership is a key issue in site-based management. Indeed, for some it has been so important that the term *site-based leadership* has replaced *site-based management*. For the purposes of this book, leadership is one component of site-based management. This is because leadership perspectives and skills are required at the

TABLE 2.1 Differences Between Management and Leadership

Management	Leadership
About predictability and order: attaining consistent results, meeting requirements	About change: changing environmental pressures, the need to be successful
Planning and budgeting: setting goals, defining detailed steps, allocating resources	Setting a direction: creating a vision and developing a strategy to make the vision a reality
Organizing and staffing: creating an organizational structure and a set of jobs, staffing, delegating responsibility, planning, and monitoring	Aligning people: communicating the new direction to those who can form coalitions that understand the vision and are committed to its achievement
Controlling and problem solving: monitoring results versus the plan, taking corrective action	Motivating and inspiring: keeping people moving in the right direction, despite major obstacles, by appealing to basic needs, values, and emotions
Controlling people by pushing them in the right direction: authority, job performance, and evaluation	Motivating people by satisfying basic human needs: achievement, sense of belonging, recognition, self-esteem, a sense of control over one's life. The ability to live up to one's ideals

central office level and by principals to support the leadership role of the site team. As will be discussed later, however, leadership alone is not enough.

The goal of leadership at all levels is the same: to help schools and individual teachers to express their expertise, creativity, and inventiveness in developing strategies to improve the quality of educational programs and services.

Unfortunately, many school districts have emphasized management to the near exclusion of leadership, and this distinction is important. Leadership and management perspectives are quite different. These differences have been discussed by Kotter (1990) and are summarized in Table 2.1.[1]

As important as leadership is to the success of site-based management, the position of this book is that both the leadership and management needs of the organization must be met. As Mauriel (1989) states, it is necessary to include discussions of how the two interrelate and support each other.[2] Especially in education, the same group or individual must frequently satisfy both management and leadership demands. The management demands of schools is an important topic

New Perspectives, Knowledge, and Skills

TABLE 2.2 Leadership Characteristics

Vision	Ability to articulate the larger purposes of the organization and to build a shared commitment among the members of the organization in the attainment of those goals
Trust	Demonstrating a real concern for the welfare of the members of the organization and an ability to deal with them in an open, honest, and consistent manner
Credibility	Being aware of the real issues and needs of different members of the organization and having the technical knowledge and skills to effectively address them
Inspiration	Being confident and optimistic about the future, challenging others to excel, and building an organizational climate in which others are supported in their personal development

and will be discussed in the following chapters on the central office, principal, and site team. To set the stage, the definition of leadership is introduced here.

Leadership is a function of the daily, concrete actions of individuals and groups. It is not a once-a-year speech and it is not dependent on the charisma of an individual. Leadership effectiveness is measured by the perceptions of others and by the extent to which leadership is ascribed to another person or group. Effective leaders exhibit the characteristics shown in Table 2.2.[3]

These characteristics become the criteria against which leaders and leadership activities will be measured to determine their success. Discussions in later chapters will focus on the behaviors required of the central office, principal, and site teams to put leadership perspectives into practice.

Creating a Shared Vision

Developing a schoolwide, shared vision is recommended as one of the major, early activities of the site team. It is an activity that will facilitate the development of the site team as a cohesive group and signal the district's change to site-based management. Creating a shared vision as a schoolwide activity will reinforce the trust, credibility, and inspiration aspects of the site team's leadership. The act of developing a shared vision together establishes, from the beginning, a collaborative relationship with the other members of the school. Participation by others will begin to build the shared commitment to its attainment.

The shared vision should be a future-oriented statement of the larger purposes and ideals to be achieved by the school staff and program. The vision statement can be organized in several ways and will be discussed later in the book. What should be stressed at this point, however, is that it should be stated in simple language and be descriptive in nature. In its simplest terms, it should describe what school is like for parents, students, and staff. This approach will allow the vision to be a working statement, one that can be translated into the daily activities, interactions, and attitudes of all members of the organization. It provides an answer to the question, "Why are we doing this?"

Generating a shared vision provides an opportunity for the whole school to look at the big picture together. Unfortunately, this is an infrequent activity in most schools. Research has shown that during the typical school day, teachers engage in virtually no professional dialogue despite the fact that this interaction and sharing with colleagues is perceived as valuable and rewarding. The daily routine is dominated by concrete concerns and activities. Teachers focus on their own role and the immediate needs of students, parents, and other staff members. The site team, however, can build into the organizational routine activities that focus on the vision and progress being made toward its attainment. This is one of the major, ongoing responsibilities of the site team.

Developing Strategic Planning Skills

Strategic planning is a particularly important process for the schools of today. The environment of schools, the demands and constraints under which schools operate, the needs of students, and the resources available to schools are in a constant state of change. One result, in response to these changes, has been an increase in the number of externally imposed requirements, standards, and programs. As the external demands on schools have increased, central office personnel have become responsible for an increasing diversity of programs that have been largely perceived as "add-ons" by building personnel. In addition, demands and requirements for increased parent and staff involvement have led to an increasing number of committees at both the district and building level. These committees tend to work independently of each other and to make isolated decisions about individual program components.

The result has been to increase demands on the time and energy of district and building personnel. Workshops, professional development activities, schedule changes, special events, and new classroom instructional units seem to expand geometrically, whereas the length of the school day and year remains relatively constant. Furthermore, although the new programs and requirements may be worthwhile and even necessary, they begin to compete with each other for the

New Perspectives, Knowledge, and Skills 13

attention of district and building personnel and often result in conflicting demands on individuals. As a result, the overriding purposes of the educational program of the school may become lost in the shuffle. As time passes, decision makers and priorities change, programs are begun and dropped, and participants lose a sense of control.

Strategic planning is a process that helps you look at where you are, where you want to go, and what it will take to get there. It allows a focus on the total school program, provides a sense of control over the future, and allows the organization to be responsive to a constantly changing environment of needs and demands.

There are six steps in the strategic planning process for schools:

1. Identify the external forces, current and future, acting on the district and its schools.

2. Define the nature of the client population and its current and future needs.

3. Clarify the values and beliefs of participants about education.

4. Create a shared vision of the future.

5. Assess the strengths and weaknesses of the program.

6. Set priorities and plan program improvements.

Creating a shared vision is at the core of strategic planning. The shared vision must be responsive to external forces, address needs of the client population, and incorporate beliefs and values about education. Furthermore, it is the basis for assessing the relative strengths and weaknesses of the educational program and identifying priorities for improvement. Planning and implementing program improvements are the means by which the shared vision becomes reality.

If the site team uses the strategic planning process from the beginning, it helps the team develop the schoolwide perspectives that significant school improvement requires. If it does not use the strategic planning process, then its decisions will be similar to previous patterns and lack overall direction and effectiveness. Although decisions about budget, staffing, and program may be made, they may not be relevant or linked to improving the total educational program of the school.

Defining New Roles

Site-based management will require central office personnel, principals, and members of site teams to adopt new roles and responsibilities. Although it is difficult to change customary patterns of behavior, these new roles will actually enhance the professional experiences of all participants. This role enhancement will stem, in part, from the leadership perspectives gained and skills acquired.

While these new roles are being learned, experience will be less effective as a guide to behavior. In this context, communication skills and listening to the needs of others will be critical. This will be particularly true in the group decision-making settings where new activities and patterns of interactions will be required. All the participants in site-based management will have to work together in an atmosphere of shared responsibility to make it work.

Shared responsibility is a key element of the new roles in site-based management and helps to define the relationship between the central office and individual schools, the principal and the site team, and the site team and the school staff.

The central office has a critical role to play in the development and operation of site-based management in schools. Whereas some advocates of site-based management see a diminished role for the central office, functioning as a "holding company" providing a few centralized services, the position of this book is that an active role is necessary.

But what role is the central office to play? Two different scenarios frequently exist, neither one of which is an effective role for the central office.[4] One is "too much" and one is "too little."

The Scenario of "Too Much"

This role is one of continued centralized control. A mistake made by some districts is to treat site-based management like other "new" programs initiated by the central office. In this approach, site-based management is rigidly defined, extensive and standardized policies and guidelines are created, and progress is monitored by the use of forms for reporting goals, objectives, and activities. Criteria for success are established by the central office. If individual schools are not making adequate progress as defined by the central office, the central office pushes a little harder for control and compliance.

In effect, the decisions made by the school are still tightly controlled, and the rhetoric of site-based management and the reality do not match. Schools become disillusioned, and their response becomes one of apathetic acceptance, meeting minimal standards for performance, going through the motions, and waiting for it to go away. (It has happened all too often.)

The Scenario of "Too Little"

Another response made by the central office has been to do just the opposite, that is, provide *no* guidance, expectations, or assistance to individual schools. Site-based management seems to be defined as "you're on your own now," or "it's something we will have to figure out as we go along." Some schools do nothing, whereas others "take the ball and run with it." They devote extensive time, energy, and effort to making it work. They make significant decisions to change their school programs, only to have the decisions vetoed by the central office because of some reason or other having to do with "districtwide needs." Site teams become angry and frustrated, trust in the central office disappears, and the school adopts the behaviors of minimal compliance. (This happens a lot too.)

It is important to note that both approaches—too much and too little—lead to the same results. Site-based management fails to be successfully implemented. The central office needs to take a middle ground approach.

The role of the central office, to be effective in site-based management, must become one of providing leadership and technical assistance to schools as they change to site-based management. Control and compliance are replaced by a service orientation where the school becomes the *internal customer* of the central office. The role of the central office focuses on two areas:

1. Providing the leadership and services necessary for schools to increase the quality of decisions about the instructional program
2. Providing the resources to facilitate the implementation of those programs

Site-based management does not eliminate the need for a school principal. The site team needs to focus on a leadership role including the decisions and activities of strategic planning. The management demands of most schools are simply too immediate and too extensive to be met without a principal. However, under site-based management, the principal will have to address both the management and leadership needs of the school. In many ways, the principal's new role will parallel that of the central office—providing leadership and services to the site team. In turn, the role of the site team is to provide leadership and assistance to the school staff.

Therefore, whereas the new roles of the central office, principal, and site team will require new activities and interactions, these are defined by the larger purposes they serve. The specifics of these new roles are discussed in the following chapters.

Enhancing the Work Environment

The success of site-based management will depend, in part, on the degree to which it makes a real difference in the daily lives of the members of the organization. It was stated in the first chapter that site-based management has the potential to lead to school improvement in two interdependent areas:

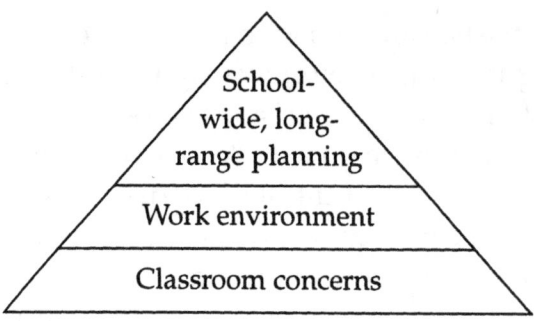

Figure 2.2. Teacher Hierarchy of Concerns

1. The quality of the educational programs and services for students, parents, and the community

2. The quality of the work environment for all members of the organization

Much of the attention thus far has been focused on the first area, improving the quality of the educational program. This is certainly intended to improve the daily lives of all members of the organization through increased levels of satisfaction and feelings of accomplishment and success. It is distinct, however, from the second area, the quality of the work environment. The work environment is defined simply as the conditions under which the members of the organization work. These conditions have a direct influence on the ability of organizational members to function effectively on a daily basis in the delivery of educational programs and services. The site team must understand that the work environment of the school is critical to the team's own success.

In site-based management, participation in decision making is intended to be a motivating factor to improve the energy, commitment, and morale of teachers as well as increase the quality of decisions about the instructional program. The hierarchy of teacher concerns, diagrammed in Figure 2.2, must be considered in discussions of motivating teachers.

Given this hierarchy of concerns, teachers will not participate effectively in instructional leadership activities unless they feel that the more basic and immediate concerns of the work environment and the classroom are satisfied.

Teachers derive their greatest job satisfaction from teaching itself, that is, interacting with students at the classroom level. This is where they look for a sense of achievement and seek status, recognition, and increased responsibility. As a result, teachers place the first priority on classroom issues such as classroom management, subject-matter knowledge, teaching strategies, curriculum materials, class preparation, and the needs and learning styles of students.

The work environment, however, can be a potential source of dissatisfaction. Teachers are typically less concerned with issues like policies and administration, supervision, and working conditions unless they fall below a given level of acceptance. The work environment then begins to interfere with teachers' preferred focus on the classroom; competes for their attention, time, and energy; and leads to what teachers perceive as "management problems."

The management problems for teachers at the classroom level include large class sizes, inadequate supplies, excessive paperwork demands, difficulties with substitute teachers, limited access to audiovisual equipment, and student absenteeism and tardiness. The management problems for teachers at the work environment level may include extra duties, excessive staff meetings, limited professional development opportunities, the poor condition of the building, poor staff relationships, a lack of administrative support, and poor communication.

The site team must recognize the priorities of teachers and understand the need to address management problems in strategic planning. If teachers are to engage in schoolwide, long-range planning in an active and committed fashion, then the site team must also address the "real issues" of the staff.

Understanding Group Dynamics

The shared decision-making component of site-based management calls for a major shift for schools in terms of who is involved in what decisions at what level in the organization. Whereas committees are certainly not a new feature of schools, their function in the past has typically been limited to specific problems and needs. Various committees are frequently limited to making recommendations to others who make the final decisions. Although committees may be broad based in representation, they traditionally operate in the existing hierarchy of authority.

Site-based management, in contrast, calls for new, broadly defined responsibilities and authority. Unfortunately, it is rarely made clear exactly how the new responsibilities and authority will be put into practice. The greatest challenge to the site team is frequently its first—defining its own role. Both the process and content of this early decision will be influenced by the needs, perspectives, and knowledge of each individual in the group. The dynamics of the group will have an effect at once. Managing the group itself will become an immediate critical issue.

There are two areas that must be addressed in understanding and influencing the dynamics of groups: stages of group development and group process skills.

It is generally agreed that groups go through several stages of development, from early "forming" activities and through periods of disruption and conflict, before they reach the stage where the group is able to be productive. Furthermore, whenever the membership of the group is changed (or the overall task of the group is altered), the team must start all over again in its development. The following sequence of activities is suggested for site teams to facilitate their movement through these stages of development:

1. Getting started
2. Learning new skills
3. Creating a shared vision
4. Setting direction and goals for school improvement
5. Planning, implementing, and reviewing strategies for improvement

Training in group process skills is widely recognized as an initial step of newly formed groups such as site teams. Training in these skills is an important group development activity, providing a shared experience base for the team as well as expertise in key skills. The training focus should include the following group of skills:

- Leadership perspectives and behaviors
- Strategic planning
- Group effectiveness skills
- Problem solving and decision making
- Planning and project management

Clarifying Accountability

The major question of site-based management for many people is: "Who is accountable to whom and for what?" How the accountability of different individuals and roles is defined and used is critical to the success of site-based management.

There are four requirements essential to successful accountability.

1. It must be defined in cooperation between the central office and the individual school site.
2. It must be communicated clearly and frequently at all levels of the organization.

3. It becomes the structure for the work of individuals and groups in their activities and interactions with others.
4. It becomes the basis on which people are evaluated.

Although the definition of accountability will vary from one setting to another because of the unique needs and issues of different districts and schools, it must be specified in terms of what individuals and groups produce and how they produce it. For example, teachers are responsible not only for what they teach but how they teach. And site teams are responsible for the decisions they make and how they reach those decisions. There are both process and content components to roles and responsibilities in site-based management.

Accountability must also take into consideration the larger organizational needs previously discussed in this chapter, for example, systemwide perspectives, leadership, vision, and strategic planning. Accountability must go beyond the specific "job" of the individual. It should take into account the larger purposes of the organization (as reflected in its vision and strategic planning) and the contribution of different groups and individuals to its accomplishment. This concept applies to the central office as well as the individual teacher.

In general, accountability in site-based management for the central office, principals, site-team members, and teachers should include the areas presented in Table 2.3.

Recommended Steps in Implementing Site-Based Management

In this chapter, nine key components have been identified that support the successful implementation of site-based management. If leadership, new roles, strategic planning, shared visions, and the other components of site-based management are to become a reality in the organization, they must become part of the language of its members and express "what is really important here." They must become part of the new ways of thinking and the new patterns of behavior. In short, they must be part of the new norms and values of the organization and be demonstrated in the daily activities of its participants.

The nine key components are an integral part of a 25-step sequence recommended for implementing site-based management. This sequence of steps begins at the central office or district level, moves to the principal level, and then focuses on the site team. We believe the success of site-based management on a districtwide basis is dependent on the completion of each step in order. There are 10 steps that the central office should complete before the individual sites begin their

TABLE 2.3 Accountability in Site-Based Management

Central office	Creating a strategic plan for the district and communicating it effectively to individual schools
	Providing the leadership and services necessary for site teams to increase the quality of decisions about instructional programs and services
	Providing the resources to facilitate the program improvement plans of the individual buildings
Site teams	Creating a shared vision of the desired educational program of the school
	Creating a strategic plan to support the attainment of the vision and to guide decisions about budget, program, and staffing
	Learning and practicing leadership and group process skills
	Evaluating the quality of the instructional program and services provided to clients
Principals	Providing leadership and technical assistance to the site team
	Supporting the shared vision and strategic plan of the site team and school
	Meeting the management needs of the school to promote a quality work environment
Teachers	Providing the site team with their knowledge and perspectives on the educational program and services of the school
	Performing their role in a manner consistent with the shared vision of the school

own implementation efforts. The five steps for the principal should be completed before the 10 steps of the site team are begun. In sum, the changes at the central office level will help principals adopt the behaviors that will in turn support the efforts of the site team.

For those schools and districts who have already begun site-based management, a thorough review of the 25 steps, introduced in Table 2.4, may provide insight into the changes that might be necessary to increase the effectiveness of the current site-based management efforts.

New Perspectives, Knowledge, and Skills

TABLE 2.4 Steps in Implementing Site-Based Management

Central Office	Principal	Site Team
Adopt a leadership perspective	Adopt a systemwide perspective	Form the site team
Assess context of change	Assess context of change	Learn new skills
Adopt strategic planning model	Implement effectiveness plan to facilitate site-based management	Adopt strategic planning model
Examine external forces	Adopt leadership behaviors	Examine external forces
Examine student needs	Define new roles and accountability	Examine student needs
Examine values, beliefs, and expectations		Examine values, beliefs, and expectations
Set overall district vision		Create a shared vision
Set expectations and parameters for site teams and principals		Assess current program and services
Identify management needs of schools		Set priorities for improvement
Create support roles for leadership and service		Plan, implement, and evaluate program improvements

This review will help districts avoid or solve the problems that have often been experienced during the implementation of site-based management. These typical problems include the following:

1. No leadership is evident at the central office level.
2. No overriding vision exists for the educational programs.

3. No coordination occurs across buildings in the district.
4. Central office/building relationship is unclear.
5. Buildings are unaware of the big picture.
6. Team meetings are inefficient and ineffective.
7. Principals are reluctant to give up control.
8. Site-based management is seen as another "add-on."

Once the problems of the current site-based management efforts have been identified, selected steps can be completed that will address the areas of concern at either the central office, principal, or site-team level. In some situations, it will be important to make those changes first at the central office level that will support the desired changes at the individual school level.

The sequence of steps may also be helpful to those districts who have begun site-based management on a limited or trial basis and who wish to (a) expand from a pilot program in a few schools, (b) grant additional decision-making authority to site teams after a successful start, or (c) use site-based management to initiate significant changes that are responses to changing conditions either inside or outside of the district.

The recommended sequence of 25 steps for implementing site-based management is the basis for Chapters 3 through 10. The final chapter provides guidelines for answering the question, "Are we making progress?"

Notes

1. Kotter (1990) discusses the differences between leadership and management in a business setting, but the distinction is valid for all settings.

2. The work by Mauriel (1989) also provides an excellent guide to planning educational change at the district level.

3. These categories were inspired by the discussions of Kouzes and Posner (1987) on what followers expect from leaders.

4. The two scenarios were derived from discussions with principals and teachers from numerous school districts about the problems of working with the central office under site-based management. Both scenarios were observed within the same district over time and with regard to different issues.

3

The Role of the Central Office

Site-based management is perceived as a "bottom-up" strategy for change, but its success requires leadership and supportive change from the top. The school district is the unit legally responsible for providing educational programs and services to the community. It must, therefore, play a continuing role to ensure compliance with different external regulations and demands that affect individual schools. From state attendance and graduation requirements to local fire and building codes, individual schools do not have a free hand. Beyond the legal requirements, professional standards and community expectations are also the responsibility of the school district.

Under site-based management, however, individual schools assume greater decision-making powers. The question for many board members and central office personnel is: "How do we meet our larger obligations and responsibilities while granting greater autonomy to schools through site-based management?" The discussion in Chapters 3, 4, and 5 are designed to answer that question by providing a new role of leadership and service for the central office.

Adopting a Leadership Perspective

The central purpose of site-based management is to increase the quality of decisions about instructional programs. By delegating decision making to the schools, it is possible to increase the flexibility of schools so they can respond to the needs of their clients and build greater staff commitment and effort in the delivery of educational programs and services. This can be accomplished only if the board and central office restructure their own efforts, moving away from an orientation of control and compliance to an orientation of leadership and service.

The goal of this leadership perspective is to allow schools and individual teachers to use their creativity as they develop strategies at the school level for program improvement. This is a significant departure from a central office role of "now do this."

We have known for some time that it is not really possible to control what occurs behind the classroom door. We have tried, however, to influence this indirectly through certification requirements and professional development activities and by setting minimal standards for both teachers and students. The quality issue has been addressed by increasing the number of externally imposed programs, guidelines, and standards. When criticism has been levied against the schools, we have responded through increased efforts of doing more of the same—issuing new controls and imposing new special-interest programs. As a result, our attention has been fragmented by multiple interests and captured by an ever-increasing demand for monitoring and ensuring compliance to attain a "satisfactory" level.

The potential of site-based management is to recognize that "quality control" really exists, and should belong, at the school level. It is the "worker on the line" who has either a positive or negative effect on quality, and it is the teacher in the classroom who makes the real difference in educational quality.

If we really want to do a better job of educating our students, then everyone will need to change the very nature of our schools. This will require an ability to

1. Alter our belief systems
2. Acquire new knowledge
3. Develop new skills
4. Change customary patterns of behavior

This is essential for all members of the organization. It is true for teachers and principals, and no less true for board members and central office personnel.

The challenge to the districtwide decision makers is to adopt a perspective of leadership and service in which the schools—teachers and principals—become the internal customers of the organization. As discussed in Chapter 2, this requires a shift from an emphasis on management behaviors to leadership behaviors. To accomplish this shift, districtwide decision makers must initiate a series of actions and communications to demonstrate vision, engender trust, establish credibility, and provide inspiration in their relationships with others. The focus of Chapters 4 and 5 will be the actions and communications that put a leadership and service orientation into practice.

Understanding the Context of Change

The districtwide planning group for site-based management, whether it is the central office or a special task force, must take into account the context of change in its implementation plans. The context of change refers to both the recent history and current circumstances of the school district and its individual schools. The response of each participant in the organization to site-based management will be influenced by its current roles, demands, relationships with others, and levels of satisfaction with current policies, programs, and procedures. Furthermore, current issues and challenges and future hopes and concerns of the district as a whole are potential influences on the implementation of site-based management.

Current Status of Site-Based Management

Part of the context of change is the current status of site-based management within the district. Has a decision already been made to adopt site-based management? Who made the decision and why? These types of questions begin to identify the history and current perceptions of site-based management in the district that need to be taken into account in planning the implementation effort.

Worksheets 1 through 4 are provided to assess the current status of site-based management within your own setting. Following the worksheets, several suggestions are provided to help the reader identify how the responses can help guide the implementation effort.

Worksheets 1 through 4 are designed to identify the current levels of participation, clarity, and support with regard to site-based management. In general, the following holds true for efforts to implement site-based management.

1. Levels of acceptance and support for site-based management across the district will be lower if it has been adopted in response to external demands rather than to internal needs.

2. Levels of acceptance and support for site-based management across the district will be lower if the decision has not included different people at different levels in the organization.

3. Clarity about site-based management across the district will be lower as fewer people are involved in the decision to adopt it.

4. The lower the levels of clarity about site-based management across the district, the lower the levels of acceptance and support.

(text continues on p. 30)

WORKSHEET 1
Reasons for Adopting Site-Based Management

Why is the district adopting site-based management?
(Check those that apply.)

Source of Influence or Pressure

_____ Pressure from external groups

_____ Initiative/pressure from district schools

_____ Desire to be competitive with other districts

_____ Means to resolve conflicts within district

_____ Perceived need to increase teacher participation

_____ Perceived need to increase parent involvement

_____ Response to cuts in central office personnel

_____ Response to state mandate or initiatives

_____ Part of districtwide reorganization plan

_____ Other _____

Larry J. Reynolds. *Successful Site-Based Management: A Practical Guide*, rev. ed. Copyright © 1997 by Corwin Press, Inc. Reprinted with permission.

WORKSHEET 2
Deciding on Site-Based Management

Who was involved in the decision
to adopt site-based management?

Groups Involved	Yes	No
School board	____	____
Superintendent	____	____
Central office administrators	____	____
Principals	____	____
Classroom teachers	____	____
Other professional staff	____	____
Parents	____	____
Other community members	____	____
Special task force	____	____
Other _____	____	____

Larry J. Reynolds. *Successful Site-Based Management: A Practical Guide*, rev. ed. Copyright © 1997 by Corwin Press, Inc. Reprinted with permission.

WORKSHEET 3
Clarity About New Roles and Responsibilities

How clearly do different groups
understand the new roles and responsibilities
of site-based management?

Group	Unclear	Clear
School board	____	____
Superintendent	____	____
Other central office	____	____
Principals	____	____
Classroom teachers	____	____
Other staff	____	____
Community members	____	____
Parents	____	____
Students	____	____

Larry J. Reynolds. *Successful Site-Based Management: A Practical Guide*, rev. ed. Copyright © 1997 by Corwin Press, Inc. Reprinted with permission.

WORKSHEET 4
Current Level of Support

Fill in the people and positions in the district who will be affected by site-based management and their current level of support for it.

People or Positions	Not Supportive	Uncertain	Supportive
_____	_____	_____	_____
_____	_____	_____	_____
_____	_____	_____	_____
_____	_____	_____	_____
_____	_____	_____	_____
_____	_____	_____	_____
_____	_____	_____	_____
_____	_____	_____	_____
_____	_____	_____	_____

Larry J. Reynolds. *Successful Site-Based Management: A Practical Guide*, rev. ed. Copyright © 1997 by Corwin Press, Inc. Reprinted with permission.

5. The lower the levels of clarity and support, the greater the need for communication by the districtwide planning group about the goals of site-based management and the process by which it will be implemented.

6. The lower the levels of initial acceptance and support for site-based management, the greater the time that will be required for the implementation effort.

It is important that the sequence of steps recommended for the implementation of site-based management be communicated to all members of the organization. The credibility and trust of the districtwide planning group will be enhanced by letting people know its intentions about site-based management before implementation efforts begin.

Current Issues and Programs

Understanding the context of change also requires that an inventory of the major issues, programs, and concerns of the district be completed. Site-based management will be a new demand on people's time and energy and it will have to compete for their attention. Various issues in the district may be perceived as priorities that need to be addressed before site-based management can be implemented. Current special programs and projects were initiated as high priorities by different individuals and groups, and extensive resources may already be committed to them. These concrete, daily, and ongoing demands are part of the context within which site-based management will be introduced.

As you plan for site-based management, you will have to answer the question, "What does site-based management have to do with all the other stuff we are doing?" The following worksheets (5, 6, and 7) are designed to help identify "the other stuff." It will also be helpful at this point to consider the existing decision-making structure of the district. Specifically, at this point, who made the decisions to put these special programs and projects into place?

Worksheets 5 through 7 are designed to provide an overview of the issues and programs currently facing the overall school district. (The information from Worksheets 5 through 7 will be used again in Chapter 5.) It may be useful to have different members of the planning group complete the inventory and then compare responses. Is everyone's listing the same? Is everyone equally aware of the same special programs and projects? Does everyone perceive the decisions about special program and projects being made in the same manner? If the lists are the same, then planning can continue. If the lists are very different, then the planning group will have to work together to create an agreed-on perception of the current situation.

The Role of the Central Office

WORKSHEET 5
Inventory of Districtwide Issues

What are the major issues at the school district level
that will influence site-based management?

Issue	Brief Description
Budget crisis	
Enrollment changes	
Change in student characteristics	
Administrative changes	
Staff turnover and changes	
Change in district priorities	
Internal building issues	
Morale and trust issues	
Opening and closing schools	
Other	

Larry J. Reynolds. *Successful Site-Based Management: A Practical Guide*, rev. ed. Copyright © 1997 by Corwin Press, Inc. Reprinted with permission.

WORKSHEET 6
Inventory of Special Programs and Projects

Identify the special programs and projects in the district that will compete for the time, energy, and focus of district and school personnel.

Program or Project	Schools Involved
1. New state or district graduation requirements	_____
2. Outcomes-based education	_____
3. Accreditation process and demands	_____
4. Whole language program	_____
5. Multicultural, gender-fair programs	_____
6. State-mandated programs	_____
7. Staff development	_____
8. Special funded projects	_____
9. Other	_____

Larry J. Reynolds. *Successful Site-Based Management: A Practical Guide*, rev. ed. Copyright © 1997 by Corwin Press, Inc. Reprinted with permission.

The Role of the Central Office

WORKSHEET 7
Inventory of Program and Project Decision Makers

For each of the special programs listed in Worksheet 6,
who was involved in the decision to proceed?

Program or Project	Decision Makers
1. _____	_____
2. _____	_____
3. _____	_____
4. _____	_____
5. _____	_____
6. _____	_____
7. _____	_____
8. _____	_____
9. _____	_____

Larry J. Reynolds. *Successful Site-Based Management: A Practical Guide*, rev. ed. Copyright © 1997 by Corwin Press, Inc. Reprinted with permission.

Planning for site-based management must have relevance to the ongoing issues, programs, and concerns of the district as a whole and of the individual school sites. If it does not, then the following is likely:

1. Individual sites will not know the expectations for or limits on their decision making. Which issues do we address? What programs do we add, continue, or drop?
2. Site teams will deal with minor decisions that have little effect on the school program because the "real" decisions have been and are still being made by others.
3. Site teams will deal with isolated pieces of the overall instructional program.
4. Site teams will make decisions and plans that run counter to district priorities and programs.
5. The site teams' decisions will compete for the time, energy, and attention of their own staff.
6. It will be increasingly difficult for the central office to maintain a knowledge of what individual schools are doing and why.

In the next chapter, a planning strategy for the central office is presented that makes site-based management the means of addressing these multiple issues and bringing order to multiple program demands. Perhaps the most essential part of this strategy is a shift away from focusing on separate, individual issues and programs to a broader, integrated perspective and vision.

4

Strategic Planning and Site-Based Management

Strategic planning is the means by which the central office can define the overall direction of the school district. Providing an overall direction is appropriate given the legal structure of public education, the fact that there are common needs among schools, the similar external demands that apply to all schools in a school district, and the similarity in the nature of teaching and learning demands across schools.

The key component of strategic planning is a vision of the future. It is targeted to the basic mission of the school district—to provide the appropriate educational programs and services required to meet the needs of its clients. Being able to create a vision of the future and to develop a shared commitment to its attainment is critical to the organizational effectiveness of the school district. It is the common thread that holds the school district together.

The vision at the central office level must be, at the minimum, shared with all of the schools in the district. It is recommended that school-level representatives (staff, parents, and students) be involved in generating the vision to provide a districtwide perspective and to help foster a shared commitment to its attainment.

One of the major problems of organizations, including schools and school districts, is that different members have different visions of what the organization should be and should do. For example, consider the following two pairs of statements.

School A: The purpose of schools is to teach basic skills.

School B: The purpose of schools is to prepare students for life.

School A: Schools should teach responsibility through a strict adherence to rules and regulations.

School B: Schools should teach responsibility through student decision making and self-directed learning.

These separate and different visions are frequently not shared or communicated between different members of the organization. Instead, they become the "silent criteria" we use in making requests, recommendations, and decisions regarding budget, program, and staffing in the schools. As a result, a lot of time and effort is wasted in the organization as people pursue their own priorities and reject the priorities of others. Teachers deny the requests of students, principals deny the requests of teachers, central office staff deny the requests of principals, and so on.

It is important to note that not everyone may agree with or heartily embrace all components of any shared vision. But it is essential for them to know "what the ballgame is." This is especially critical when schools are changing in response to the demands from their environment, new teaching and learning priorities are being adopted, and new norms and values are being established within the larger professional community. Communicating the vision is essential to the establishment of credibility and the evolution of trust, two of the core dimensions of leadership.

The vision is also the key to the inspiration dimension of leadership. It is a statement of what we believe, what we stand for, and what we think is important. The vision provides the individuals in the organization a sense of a larger purpose and a vehicle for understanding how their efforts contribute to the overall success of the organization.

The Strategic Planning Model

Given the goal to decentralize decision making through site-based management, we have made changes in the general strategic planning model we presented in Chapter 2. Under site-based management, the strategic planning model is different for the central office than it is for individual schools. In this chapter, the first four steps in strategic planning for the central office are examined. These steps are diagrammed in Figure 4.1.

Strategic Planning

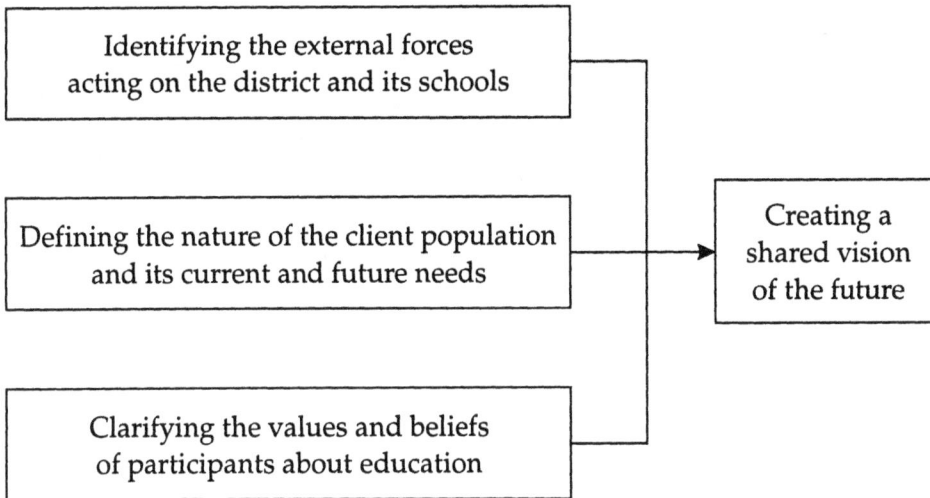

Figure 4.1. First Four Steps in District-Level Strategic Planning

External Forces

The first step in strategic planning is to identify the external forces (current and future) that will influence the range and nature of programs, services, and clients that will be included in the district's educational program. The vision of the school district should be idealistic, optimistic, and ambitious, but it must also be grounded in reality. In short, the vision must be responsive to external forces.

External forces can emanate from a variety of sources. The categories listed in Table 4.1 may be helpful to use as you list your own categories. A slightly different set of categories has been developed by Mauriel (1989) and is an excellent reference for thinking about external forces.

Worksheet 8 is provided to serve as a guide in the analysis of your own situation.

TABLE 4.1 Categories of External Forces

Financial trends	The economic decline, stability, or growth of the district; changes in the tax base; status of excess levies; types and levels of state funding; and so on
Community values and demands	Attitudes toward athletics, gifted and talented programs, minority-group needs, community education, basic-skills instruction, child-care programs, discipline, college preparation, and so on
Federal and state funding and programs	Changes in programs such as parent education, nutrition, child care, length of the school year, health care, graduation requirements, teacher training, multicultural programs, and drug and tobacco education
Demographics and enrollment trends	Changes in the demographics of the community such as growth, move-in and move-out rates, family values, education levels and aspirations, and distributions of school-age students
Professional standards and recommendations	Current position of professional and curriculum-centered groups on educational practices such as site-based management, outcomes-based education, cooperative learning, math and science guidelines, and so on

Strategic Planning

WORKSHEET 8
External Forces: Current and Future

List below the major conditions, decisions, and trends that have a high probability of influencing the educational programs, services, and clients of the school district.

Financial trends _____
_____
_____
_____

Community values and demands _____
_____
_____
_____

Federal and state programs _____
_____
_____
_____

Demographics and enrollment _____
_____
_____
_____

Professional standards and recommendations _____
_____
_____
_____

Larry J. Reynolds. *Successful Site-Based Management: A Practical Guide,* rev. ed. Copyright © 1997 by Corwin Press, Inc. Reprinted with permission.

Needs of Students (Current and Future)

The second step in strategic planning is to examine both the current and future needs of students. First, the vision of the school needs to meet the current needs of students while they are attending the schools of the district. If the nature of the student body is changing, then these needs will be different than they have been in the past and different than we may either be comfortable with or prepared for. For example, children entering kindergarten may not have the level of development or language skills that has existed previously in the district.

Second, the nature of our society and the world of work is changing, and the knowledge and skills students must acquire to be successful in the future are different than they have been in the past. Again, our own knowledge, skills, teaching strategies, and comfort level may not be consistent with the new knowledge and skills we must now focus on. For example, our familiarity with technology or teaching higher-level thinking skills as well as our program materials may be limited. We will need to examine not only the nature of these needs but also the implications for teachers and programs.

Worksheets 9 and 10 are provided to examine the current and future needs of students in your setting.

Strategic Planning

WORKSHEET 9
Students' Current Needs and Implications

List the characteristics of the students and their current needs when entering and attending district schools.

Characteristics of Students	Needs of Students

What are the implications of these needs for teachers in the classroom and the educational programs and services provided by the schools?

Implications for Teachers	Implications for Programs

Larry J. Reynolds. *Successful Site-Based Management: A Practical Guide*, rev. ed. Copyright © 1997 by Corwin Press, Inc. Reprinted with permission.

WORKSHEET 10
Students' Future Needs and Implications

List the types of knowledge and skills students will
require when they graduate from district schools.

1. _____
2. _____
3. _____
4. _____
5. _____

What are the implications of these needs for teachers in the classroom
and the educational programs and services provided by the schools?

Implications for Teachers	*Implications for Programs*
1. _____	1. _____
2. _____	2. _____
3. _____	3. _____
4. _____	4. _____
5. _____	5. _____

Larry J. Reynolds. *Successful Site-Based Management: A Practical Guide*, rev. ed. Copyright © 1997 by Corwin Press, Inc. Reprinted with permission.

Strategic Planning 43

Values, Beliefs, and Expectations

The third step in strategic planning is to specify the values, beliefs, and expectations we hold for each other. Each of us has formed, through life experience, a set of values, beliefs, and expectations that serve as basic assumptions about the world and what is "right." These assumptions, conscious or not, guide our reactions to people and events around us; how we think about them, and what we do in response. It is critical, especially when our decisions affect the lives of others, that we are as clear as possible about our own values and that they are shared openly with others.

Institutions, such as schools, also hold and operate based on a set of usually unspoken beliefs, norms, and implicit rules. Of all institutions, schools must explore and define what they stand for and then build programs and daily interactions among people that help fulfill those beliefs and values.

Worksheet 11 is provided to examine your own values, beliefs, and expectations.

WORKSHEET 11
Values, Beliefs, and Expectations

Below, write about your basic values, beliefs, and expectations about students, staff members, the nature of the interactions among students and staff, and the role of teachers and the school in the education of students.

Students:

Staff members:

Interactions among students and staff:

Role of teachers:

Role of the school:

Larry J. Reynolds. *Successful Site-Based Management: A Practical Guide*, rev. ed. Copyright © 1997 by Corwin Press, Inc. Reprinted with permission.

TABLE 4.2 Definition of the Three Vision Categories

Organizational climate	What behaviors, activities, and interactions make up the daily life of the school. What defines the "personality" of the school as a place to learn, work, and visit.
Program plan	How students and teachers are arranged for instruction. How you use requirements and electives, schedules, magnet programs, classes, counseling, advisers, teaming, curriculum integration, and support staff to structure the program. The outcome goals desired, such as critical thinking, problem solving, creativity, and basic knowledge and skills.
Classroom interaction	How you view students and learning in terms of both process and content. Includes considerations of student learning styles, self-concept, success, interactions, and activities in instruction.

The Vision

The value and purpose of a vision statement was described at the beginning of this chapter. We have defined vision as a series of statements that describe what the organization is trying to accomplish through its specific programs, roles, and activities and interactions among its participants. It is a goal-oriented statement that provides a picture of the future. The vision is a "guide to action" that presents the organization in its best light. And the vision must be comprehensive.

A number of different articles and books have been written in the area of school effectiveness that provide categories to use in a "total picture" approach. We suggest the use of three categories that focus on the overall school environment, educational programs, and services, and what goes on in classrooms. The three categories are defined in Table 4.2.

These categories seem to make sense given the frequent specific focus of change efforts in education. Outcomes-based education is a means of program organization, peer tutoring is designed to affect classroom interactions, and several programs are keyed to improving school climate.

A second question in generating a vision statement is: "How specific or general should the statements be?" They should be specific enough to serve as a guide to individual schools as they develop their own more specific vision, program decisions, and daily activities. The vision described in Table 4.3 may be helpful even though we feel it is certainly inappropriate considering the current demands and expectations for public education. Although the statements are brief, they do create an image of what the school would be like for its participants.

TABLE 4.3 Sample Vision

Organizational climate	1. Show up on time. 2. Do as you're told. 3. Don't rock the boat.
Program plan	1. Teaching is organized by "essential subjects." 2. Teaching focus is on learning "facts." 3. Textbooks provide the vehicle for learning. 4. Teachers work alone. 5. Teaching is done by large-group instruction. 6. All learning is sequential. 7. Success of the teacher is measured by "finishing the book."
Classroom interaction	1. Role of the teacher is to dispense expertise in a set body of knowledge. 2. Role of students is to sit, listen, and memorize. 3. Learning is an individual activity. 4. Students compete with each other for grades. 5. Student success is measured by a grade. 6. A quiet classroom is a good classroom. 7. Some students won't be successful.

Worksheet 12 is provided on the next page as a guide in generating vision statements by individuals and groups.

WORKSHEET 12
Vision Categories

In the space below, indicate your ideas of the ideal school and program. Use short statements that describe what it is like for parents, students, and staff.

Organizational climate: What behaviors, activities, and interactions make up the daily life of the school. What defines the "personality" of the school as a place to learn, work, and visit.

Program plan: How students and staff are arranged for instruction. How you use electives, requirements, schedules, magnets, classes, counseling, advisers, teaming, curriculum integration, and support staff to structure the program. The outcome goals desired such as critical thinking, problem solving, creativity, and basic knowledge and skills.

Classroom interactions: How you view students and learning in terms of both process and content. Includes considerations of student learning styles, self-concept, success, interactions, and activities in instruction.

Larry J. Reynolds. *Successful Site-Based Management: A Practical Guide,* rev. ed. Copyright © 1997 by Corwin Press, Inc. Reprinted with permission.

Checking the Vision

Once the vision is completed, it should be compared to the information generated as external forces; student needs; and values, beliefs, and expectations.

- Is the vision responsive to external forces?
- Does the vision meet student needs?
- Is the vision consistent with educational values and beliefs?

Not all of the information generated in examining these areas needs to be incorporated into the vision. Some information, particularly the external forces, may dictate the resources, flexibility, and even specific strategies needed to attain the vision in planning efforts. But the vision must be accurate and realistic if it is to serve as a guide to action.

Next Steps

Once the districtwide vision is generated, planning can begin at the district level to attain the vision using site-based management as a strategy. The role of the district will be twofold:

1. Providing the leadership and services necessary to assist site teams in increasing the quality of their decisions about educational programs and services
2. Providing the resources to facilitate the program improvement plans created at the various schools

The next chapter will focus on this second part of strategic planning at the district level.

5

Putting the Vision to Work

It is at this point that the district must decide how much autonomy to give the site teams in deciding on the priorities and strategies to attain the districtwide vision. This decision will reflect either the district's maintenance of a management orientation or the adoption of a leadership orientation.

Site-based management with a traditional management role of the central office would be as follows:

1. The district generates a vision of the future.
2. The district reviews the current reality in terms of the vision.
3. The district selects priorities as districtwide goals.
4. The district requires schools to submit for approval detailed plans to attain the goals.
5. The district holds schools accountable for compliance with plans and evaluates program effectiveness across the district.

The site-based management with the adoption of a leadership role of the central office would be as follows:

1. The district generates an overall vision of the future.
2. Individual school sites generate a shared vision at their level.
3. School sites review the current reality in their own setting.
4. School sites set their own priorities given their needs.
5. School sites plan, implement, and review program improvement efforts.

It is likely that different school districts will vary in the extent to which they move from the traditional central office management role of control and compliance (first example above) to the leadership role under site-based management (second example above). The danger of the first approach is that the district may define a large number of goals and a complex planning and approval process so that the district goals and their attainment become the *only* decisions and activities the site team has time to accomplish.

An additional factor to be considered at the district level is the varying needs of the schools across the district. Public relations may be a strength of some schools, a weakness of others. Teacher involvement in decision making may be high in certain buildings, absent in others. Discipline may be good here but poor there. Reading scores may be significantly higher in some schools. Teacher morale may be a problem with one school, excellent across town. Different issues in different schools may need to be addressed at different levels. Districtwide goals and programs may not only fail to match the greatest needs of a school but may also drain away the time, energy, and resources needed to address school-centered needs.

As the central office limits the autonomy and discretion of the site team, the following will also occur:

1. A decrease in the use of the vision at either the district or school level as a guide to action and decision making

2. A decrease in the level of involvement and commitment to site-based management at the building level

3. A decrease in the likelihood of the school site demonstrating leadership and initiative in making other program improvement plans and decisions

The appropriate balance between districtwide goals and priorities and site-level goals and priorities is a tricky one. The central office *can* express leadership by setting districtwide goals. In general, the more inclusive districtwide planning becomes by involving participants from across the district, the more likely districtwide goals will be perceived as valid for individual sites. In some instances, districtwide goals and programs may be dictated by external forces and become givens for everyone, district-level and school-level participants as well. Furthermore, the schools in the district do have common needs in areas such as teaching and learning, equipment and materials, and professional development.

As discussed in Chapter 2, the central office must find a balance between providing too much or too little structure and direction to school sites. This balance must be addressed during the strategic planning process of the central office and prior to the time that the school site teams begin to function. Therefore, after the

Putting the Vision to Work 51

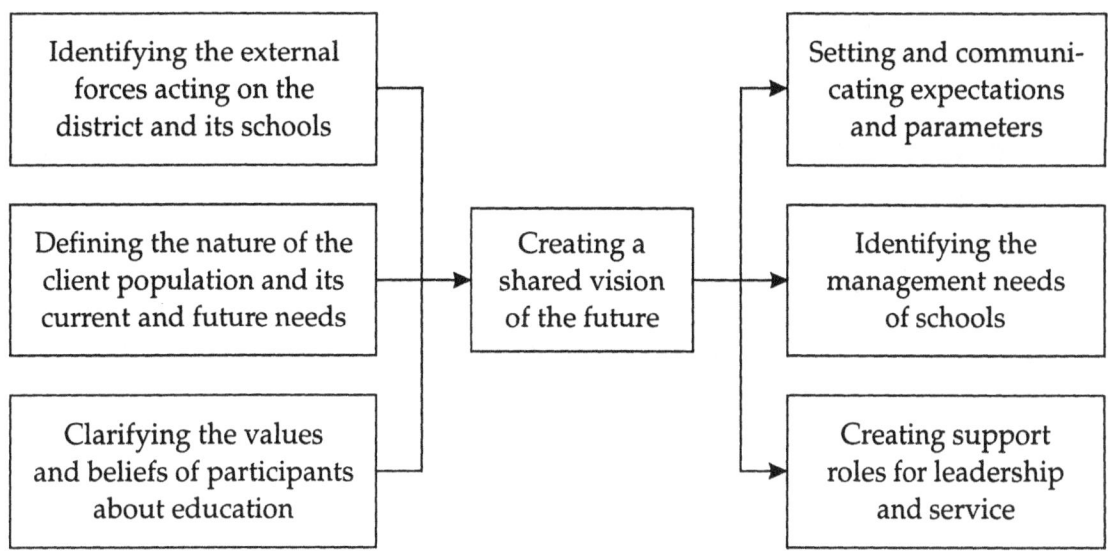

Figure 5.1. District-Level Strategic Planning Model

districtwide planning group has created the district-level vision, it must then define how the central office will help the individual schools to attain that vision within their own setting. The final three steps in the strategic planning model for the central office are

1. Setting and communicating expectations and parameters for site teams and principals
2. Identifying the management needs of schools
3. Creating support roles for leadership and service

The complete strategic planning model for the central office is presented in Figure 5.1.

Setting and Communicating Expectations and Parameters

The districtwide decision makers should specify and communicate the expectations and parameters under which the site teams will operate *before* the site teams are even formed. This will facilitate the development of the central office leadership role. By knowing "the rules of the game" at the start, both site teams and central office personnel can focus their energies appropriately. This also provides prospective site-team members with an understanding early on of what the site team will do and gives the potential members an opportunity to make an informed choice about participation.

The expectations and parameters for individual school sites fall into the following areas:

1. The criteria for evaluation of the overall efforts of schools under site-based management
2. The steps in implementing site-based management that will be followed by principals and site teams across the district
3. The expected benefits of adopting site-based management in individual schools and across the district
4. The types of budget, staffing, and program decisions that will be made by the site teams as part of their strategic planning
5. The required districtwide goals and programs that will be adopted by schools across the district

Criteria for Evaluation

It will become easier for district-level decision makers to grant autonomy and discretion to individual schools if the criteria by which the efforts of schools will be evaluated are defined before the fact. As stated earlier, the vision is the key component of strategic planning and the criteria by which the quality of the educational program is measured. The vision, however, is meaningless unless it is supported by the concrete attitudes, activities, and interactions of the members of the organization. Therefore, it is appropriate for the board and central office not only to set an overall vision for the educational program of the district but also to specify the criteria by which the overall efforts of the schools are to be judged in attaining the vision under site-based management.

Furthermore, the organizational effectiveness of schools is ultimately dependent on the attitudes, activities, and interactions of all members of the organization. Although the principal and site team have key roles to play in the implementation of site-based management, their efforts alone cannot produce excellence. It is critical, therefore, that all members of the organization be aware of the expectations and goals of site-based management and how the school is to be judged.

For example, school effectiveness might be evidenced by the following:

1. Developing a strategic plan that includes a shared vision of excellence in the desired educational program
2. Demonstrating leadership and initiative in continuous program improvement efforts to attain the vision

Putting the Vision to Work 53

3. Creating an effective work environment
4. Determining organizational arrangements to maximize human and financial resources
5. Solving problems at the school level
6. Evaluating program effectiveness in terms of the vision and student success
7. Functioning in compliance within the appropriate legal and policy requirements and guidelines

Steps in Implementing

These steps have been specified earlier for both principals and site teams and are the focus of the following chapters. The point to be made here, however, is that these steps are a "given." They provide a common process across all schools, allowing the central office to provide a common set of resources to facilitate the development of site-based management. And by requiring all schools to submit strategic plans, the central office retains a common means to monitor program improvement efforts.

Expected Benefits

The districtwide decision-making group will need to specify the expected benefits of site-based management. Because site-based management is a comprehensive change strategy, a variety of benefits may be perceived by different participants. Worksheet 13 is provided as a tool for surveying various participants and for suggesting the multiple benefits that are desired. This information can then be used by the central office to state its intentions for adopting site-based management across the district.

WORKSHEET 13
Expectations for Site-Based Management

Indicate the desired effect of site-based management on each of the following items.

Potential Benefits	Potential Effect			
	(low) 1	2	3	4 (high)
Greater principal awareness of issues and concerns	____	____	____	____
Greater staff awareness of issues and concerns	____	____	____	____
Greater staff awareness of student needs	____	____	____	____
More effective response to student needs	____	____	____	____
More innovation and change	____	____	____	____
More staff involvement in decision making	____	____	____	____
Better communication among staff	____	____	____	____
Greater staff cohesiveness	____	____	____	____
Increased ownership of program by staff	____	____	____	____
Increased staff awareness of effective programs	____	____	____	____
Improved attainment of student outcomes	____	____	____	____
More parent involvement in decision making	____	____	____	____
Increased support from parents	____	____	____	____

Larry J. Reynolds. *Successful Site-Based Management: A Practical Guide*, rev. ed. Copyright © 1997 by Corwin Press, Inc. Reprinted with permission.

Types of Budget, Staffing, and Program Decisions

The fourth area for the districtwide decision makers to specify to the site teams is the decision areas that are delegated to them. It is important to remember that the districtwide strategic planning process and the vision are to be used by all site teams to identify priorities for their program improvement. Specific decisions within the general areas of budget, staffing, and program, however, will be made by the site team to attain the site's goals in program improvement. Any district limitations should be carefully spelled out ahead of time.

Worksheet 14 is provided as a tool to guide discussions about these decision areas and communicating the expectations and parameters to site teams.

WORKSHEET 14
Expectations Concerning Decision Making

For each of the decision areas listed below, indicate the level of decision-making authority you see for the site teams of individual schools.

Decision Area	Decision Authority			
	Authority to Decide on Own	Decide With District Review	Recommend to District for Approval	District Decision
Distribution of allocated budget for staff positions	_____	_____	_____	_____
Distribution of allocated budget for supplies and materials	_____	_____	_____	_____
Identification of student and program needs	_____	_____	_____	_____
Identification of goals and directions for school improvement efforts	_____	_____	_____	_____
Identification of learner outcomes for students	_____	_____	_____	_____
Identification of the curriculum and the needed instructional strategies	_____	_____	_____	_____
Identification of policies and procedures, for example, discipline, attendance, homework	_____	_____	_____	_____
Identification of performance indicators of student learning and success	_____	_____	_____	_____
Distribution of staff development moneys	_____	_____	_____	_____
Selection of new staff members	_____	_____	_____	_____
Participation in staff evaluation	_____	_____	_____	_____
Identification of priorities for building maintenance and improvement	_____	_____	_____	_____

Larry J. Reynolds. *Successful Site-Based Management: A Practical Guide,* rev. ed. Copyright © 1997 by Corwin Press, Inc. Reprinted with permission.

Required Districtwide Goals and Programs

The fifth area of expectations and parameters to be identified by district-level decision makers are the specific programs and activities that are required by the district. There may be either continuing or new requirements. These should be clearly identified, however, by their relationship to the districtwide vision and by the decision makers involved. (It should be helpful at this point to review Worksheets 6 and 7.) The districtwide vision should be used as a means to identify those that are not consistent with the vision or are not having the desired effect on student success. In this way, the use of the vision as a guide to action will be reinforced.

These worksheets and programs should now be reviewed, revised, and communicated. Worksheet 15 is provided as a tool to list the program parameters stemming from district goals and priorities and to serve as a communication tool in specifying program parameters to individual schools.

WORKSHEET 15
Required Districtwide Programs

Indicate in the space below which districtwide programs are required by the district to be implemented in the individual school sites. Indicate who has the decision-making authority for the program. Also indicate which components of the districtwide vision the program is designed to meet.

Program	Schools Involved	Decision Maker(s)	Relationship to Vision
1.			
2.			
3.			
4.			
5.			
6.			

Larry J. Reynolds. *Successful Site-Based Management: A Practical Guide*, rev. ed. Copyright © 1997 by Corwin Press, Inc. Reprinted with permission.

Putting the Vision to Work 59

Identifying the Management Needs of Schools

As discussed earlier, the leadership capability of the central office will be influenced by its credibility with participants at the school level. Discussions of a vision of future excellence will fall on deaf ears if the real needs of the schools are not being met. As stated earlier, leadership will not emerge in an organization that is poorly managed. Therefore, the central office must focus on its management role as an initial step in establishing its leadership role. Furthermore, by addressing the management needs of the schools, site teams will be more likely to focus on instructional issues rather than the work environment and management needs of the school. (See earlier discussion in Chapter 2 on the work environment and the hierarchy of teacher attention.)

It is recommended that a survey be done of the management issues and problems on a school-by-school basis. This can be accomplished by central office staff working with the principals. In fact, it has been listed as one of the expectations for the principal's role in site-based management. It is not necessary to make this an exhaustive written process. It can be conducted through an interview process thereby avoiding an increase in the paperwork demands from the central office.

The purpose of this activity should be clearly stated to individual sites: to assist the administration in providing leadership and services to solve the management problems of the school sites so that the new site teams can focus on instructional leadership. It is important to note that the management problems may stem from either central office or building causes.

It is not enough, however, merely to survey the problems. As will be discussed in the next section on new roles for the central office, the central office can build trust and credibility only by actually having someone in charge of identifying and meeting the management needs of schools.

Worksheet 16 is provided to suggest a way of summarizing the management needs through the survey.

WORKSHEET 16
Central Office Assistance With Management Needs

Indicate which schools have the following types of problems in the district.

Management Issue	Schools Needing Assistance
Building maintenance	_____
Transportation	_____
Discipline policies	_____
Workshop reimbursements	_____
Budget cycle	_____
School calendar	_____
Special events	_____
Security	_____
Grade reporting	_____
Parent conferences	_____
Purchasing and delivery	_____
Attendance policies	_____
Other	_____

Larry J. Reynolds. *Successful Site-Based Management: A Practical Guide*, rev. ed. Copyright © 1997 by Corwin Press, Inc. Reprinted with permission.

Putting the Vision to Work 61

Creating Support Roles for Leadership and Service

As stated previously, the mission of the central office in implementing site-based management is twofold:

1. To provide the leadership and services necessary for the schools to increase the quality of decisions about the instructional program
2. To provide the resources to facilitate program improvement efforts

Central office staff can identify the services and resources needed in site-based school improvement efforts by asking the schools the following list of questions:

1. What do you want to do?
2. What do you have to do?
3. What human resources do you need?
4. What program resources do you need?
5. What problems are you having?
6. What do you need to know?
7. What is the environment you require?

These questions become the new focus of the central office when assisting schools in their school improvement efforts. Furthermore, the central office roles can be formally structured to help site teams address these questions. These roles can be designed for any level or positions in the district. We have used the title Assistant Superintendent to indicate their importance. The new roles are matched with the questions from above and presented in Table 5.1.

The central office support roles suggested in Table 5.1 provide an illustration of a change in the roles and responsibilities of the central office from a control and compliance orientation toward the schools to an orientation of leadership and service. How these roles are distributed among central office staff is not critical; they can be handled by differing numbers of people and combinations of roles. But all the functions and activities must be incorporated in some way for the central office to be prepared to make site-based management succeed.

Assigning people to these roles should be based on the individual's supportive attitude toward site-based management, previous levels of trust and credibility in interactions with school site personnel, and the level of leadership expertise and

(text continued on p. 64)

TABLE 5.1 New Service Roles of the Central Office

Focus Question for School-Centered Service Role	New Position
What do you want to do?	Assistant Superintendent of Shared Visions
What do you have to do?	Assistant Superintendent of Paperwork and Compliance
What human resources do you need?	Assistant Superintendent of Personal Growth and Development
What program resources do you need?	Assistant Superintendent of Promising Practices
What problems are you having?	Assistant Superintendent of Problem Solving
What do you need to know?	Assistant Superintendent of Information and Communication
What is the environment you require?	Assistant Superintendent of Human Environments

NOTE: The responsibilities of each of these Assistant Superintendent roles are defined as follows:

Shared Visions

1. Is responsible for seeing that the district-level shared vision is part of the working language of the school district and serves as the overriding goal in decisions
2. Works directly with district-level decision-making groups and school site teams
3. Provides technical assistance and training in strategic planning processes
4. Assists school site teams in preparation of strategic plans
5. Helps evaluate districtwide programs in terms of districtwide vision

Paperwork and Compliance

1. Is responsible for monitoring and communicating external demands and requirements for the operations, programs, and services of the district and individual schools
2. Coordinates district reporting and paperwork requirements across the district
3. Creates a yearly calendar of decision deadlines for site teams to coordinate program, budget, and staffing decisions across the district
4. Works directly with site teams in examining external forces and district parameters during the planning process
5. Gathers information on external forces and trends that will shape the district's required programs and services in the future

Personal Growth and Development

1. Is responsible for identifying the professional development needs of all employees of the district to facilitate achieving the district and individual site visions
2. Identifies the needs across the district for training in new skills to support site-based management, for example, leadership and group process skills

3. Works with and provides support to principals as they assume their new roles as required by site-based management, for example, motivation, coaching, and customer focus
4. Coordinates professional development activities across the district to address common needs among individual schools
5. Identifies and/or trains people inside the district who can provide workshops and coaching support within the district

Promising Practices

1. Is responsible for providing assistance to site teams in locating new strategies for program improvements
2. Identifies and develops the expertise of master teachers within the district to demonstrate and teach promising practices
3. Provides status and recognition to school staff who demonstrate leadership and initiative in implementing program improvement ideas and practices

Problem Solving

1. Is responsible for the central office's commitment to address the management needs of individual sites
2. Develops a level of trust with individual schools that engages people in problem identification and problem solving rather than passivity and blaming others
3. Provides training to principals and site teams in problem-solving strategies
4. Works directly with principals and site teams in problem-solving strategies
5. Works as problem-solving link between district-level and school-level personnel

Information and Communication

1. Is responsible for ensuring that decision making in the district is based on accurate and complete information
2. Serves as a communication link between the central office and schools so that the central office has a valid picture of "what it is like in the schools"
3. Responds to site-team questions about the site team's new role requirements and decision-making authority by getting immediate answers from the central office
4. Reinforces customer orientation of schools by creating a flow of information to and from the community with regard to educational programs and services

Human Environments

1. Is responsible for creating an effective work environment for all participants in the organization—parents, students, and staff
2. Examines the different settings where people spend their time by asking three questions: (a) Is it safe? (b) Is it comfortable? and (c) Is it pleasant, engaging, inspiring, motivating, and learner friendly?
3. Moves beyond a maintenance perspective by working with site teams to identify ways to enhance the organizational climate of schools
4. Works with district nonteaching personnel (custodians, bus drivers, clerical staff, and cafeteria staff) to create a customer service orientation to the schools and community
5. Ensures status and recognition are given to support staff in their creation of a supportive work environment

group process skills. And to develop trust and credibility for site-based management, the district will have to demonstrate its commitment to site-based management with more than words. Visions and strategic plans are a good start, but it will require highly visible changes in the roles and responsibilities of central office staff to support the emergence of site-based management in the schools.

Accountability

In Chapters 4 and 5 we have focused on the strategic planning efforts and outputs of the district-level decision makers that will facilitate the success of site-based management. Furthermore, these products need to be specified and communicated to principals and site teams, ideally, before site-based management activities begin at the building level. The outputs described are as follows:

1. Identifying the external forces acting on the district
2. Documenting the current and future needs of students
3. Stating values and beliefs about education
4. Creating a shared vision of the future
5. Clarifying expectations and parameters for schools
6. Addressing the management needs of schools
7. Creating the support roles for leadership and service

These are the outputs that the central office should be held accountable for by the schools. Furthermore, they demonstrate from the beginning the changes that site-based management brings to the usual patterns of accountability.

The typical hierarchy of organizations with a top-down management structure calls for accountability as a down-up process. Teachers are accountable to principals, principals are accountable to the central office, and central office personnel are accountable to the board. Under site-based management, accountability becomes a two-way interaction. The central office is accountable to the schools for certain outputs, and the schools are accountable to the central office for others. In short, the responsibility for the success of site-based management is shared among the central office, the principal, and the site team.

In the next chapter, we will focus on the role of the principal and how the principal is the key to the success of site-based management. For some principals, site-based management will be a natural extension of their current values and patterns of behavior. They will have many of the requisite skills and much of the knowledge required for implementing site-based management in their schools.

Putting the Vision to Work 65

For others, site-based management will be less familiar and more uncomfortable. And for still others, site-based management will be a significant, disturbing, and perhaps threatening change.

This range of readiness and ease of adoption is typical under most situations requiring significant change. The central office can help to maximize the effectiveness of all principals by doing the following:

- Demonstrating the district's commitment to site-based management by making changes in the central office roles, activities, and outputs
- Making the expectations for the behavior of the principals in site-based-managed schools clear and holding principals accountable for meeting those expectations
- Providing immediate status and recognition to those who show initiative and success in the change to site-based management

In sum, the direction and support provided by the district must be clear and consistent. And it must clearly communicate the new set of expectations regarding the principal's role in a site-based management system. The central office cannot merely tell the principal, "Do it, make it work."

In Chapter 6, the perspectives and behaviors considered essential for principals to be effective leaders in successfully establishing site-based management in their schools will be presented.

6

The Principal
The Key to Success

The building principal, more than any other single individual, will determine the success or failure of site-based management at the building level. With the principal's active support and leadership, site-based management can be an effective strategy for school improvement. The increased autonomy of the school under site-based management can provide the following potential opportunities:

- Greater flexibility and control in school improvement efforts
- Greater use of the knowledge and skills of organizational members
- Increased involvement, ownership, and commitment among organizational members
- Increased quality of decisions about the instructional program of the school

These are only opportunities, however. Without the principal's positive action and support, site-based management will not be effective and these opportunities will be missed.

The opportunity provided by site-based management also rests with the simple reality that there is a limit to what the principal can accomplish in the way of school improvement through a traditional approach of control and compliance. Although policies and procedures can be imposed, they tend to focus on the acceptable *minimal* standards. Site-based management, however, is a strategy to *maximize* the effectiveness of all the members of the organization. Therefore, whereas the shared decision-making component of site-based management requires the principal to share power in some areas, it also provides the principal

The Principal: The Key to Success 67

additional human resources and commitment to attain an improved school program.

Rather than diminishing the role of the principal, site-based management actually enhances it. However, it also calls for a more complex and sophisticated role of the principal. The principal's task is now to motivate, advise, and coach others, rather than controlling them. The principal's role becomes one of facilitating the efforts of others, rather than directing them. The principal must now also lead the school into the future, rather than only managing the status quo.

The success of site-based management at the building level also depends on the principal's ability to address the nine components of success (introduced in Chapter 2).

1. Adopting a systemwide perspective
2. Understanding the context of change
3. Developing leadership perspectives and skills
4. Creating a shared vision
5. Developing strategic planning skills
6. Defining new roles
7. Enhancing the work environment
8. Understanding group dynamics
9. Clarifying accountability

These essential components provided a guide for the perspectives, activities, and outputs of the districtwide effort (described in Chapters 3 through 5) and will provide a guide for the perspectives, activities, and outputs of the successful principal. The focus of this chapter is on the first three steps of the principal in implementing site-based management:

1. Adopting a systemwide perspective
2. Understanding the context of change
3. Increasing organizational effectiveness

Adopting a Systemwide Perspective

To effectively implement site-based management, the principal will have to adopt a systemwide perspective at two levels. The first is to review the school's role in the overall effort of the district to implement site-based management (the external system). The second is to adopt a schoolwide view of the principal's own building (the internal system).

The External System

A critical point in the effort by the district to implement site-based management is when it "hands off the ball" to the individual schools. It is paramount that school personnel understand the following:

- The district's intentions in adopting site-based management
- The strategic planning of the district in preparation for site-based management
- The outputs of the district planning that specify the expectations, parameters, and support roles for the implementation effort
- The timeline the district envisions for the creation of site teams, their development, and their assumption of decision-making responsibilities

If this understanding does not exist, the principal must insist that the district demonstrate its commitment to site-based management by immediately communicating to the staff the information listed above. This is essential to build the trust and credibility of the district with school personnel and to reinforce the legitimacy of the principal in undertaking the actions necessary to support site-based management in the building.

A second step for the principal is to review the parameters on the decision-making autonomy of the school. The following questions are appropriate:

- Are the guidelines and parameters so restrictive that site-based decision making is not worth the effort?
- Are the expectations so vague that the principal and site team have no idea what it is they are to accomplish?

If the answer to either question is yes, then the principal will have to seek clarity from the central office before he or she can effectively proceed. (See the discussion in Chapter 2 on defining new roles.)

The Internal System

The principal must also develop a school-specific or schoolwide perspective. Although all the schools in the district may share common characteristics, each school will still have its own uniqueness. It may be in terms of size, student population, program (as in different magnet schools), staff characteristics, or any number of other factors that give it a distinct reputation or personality. As a result, the principal will have to function as a translator, that is, taking the districtwide expectations and parameters for site-based management and integrating them into what is valid and necessary for his or her own school to attain the districtwide vision.

Understanding the Context of Change

Although it is generally accepted that site-based management will vary from school to school, the principal of each building is faced with a number of initial questions. How will site-based management be received in my school? What factors will influence its potential success? What does site-based management have to do with all the other things we are trying to do? How do I fit it in with all the existing demands on my time?

The answers to these questions lie, in part, in the current situation in the building with regard to four areas:

1. The current issues and problems facing the principal and school
2. The major programs and changes that are already under way that will compete for the time, energy, and commitment of the principal and staff
3. The existing decision-making structure and activities of the school
4. The principal's current activities and use of time

It is important for the principal to do an inventory or "building profile" early on in the process focusing on these four areas of influence on the success of site-based management in his or her school. This inventory will give the principal a framework to use in interpreting and applying the discussions and guidelines presented in the rest of this chapter to his or her own specific school setting.

The following worksheets examine these four areas.

- Worksheet 17 looks at the major issues and problems facing the school.
- Worksheet 18 looks at the major programs and projects under way.
- Worksheet 19 looks at the current decision-making and advisory structure of the school.
- Worksheet 20 looks at the principal's current use of time and activity patterns.

WORKSHEET 17
Principal's Survey of Major Issues and Problems

Briefly describe the major issues and problems facing your school and which group (or groups) are most concerned. Some of the issues may be similar to those of other schools in the district, and others may be unique to your school. (Examples might include budget cuts, staffing cuts, changes in students' characteristics, administrative changes, enrollment growth or decline, student safety, instructional program issues, or staff relationships.)

Concerned Group	Major Issues and Problems	Brief Description
Central office	_____	_____
	_____	_____
	_____	_____
	_____	_____
Staff	_____	_____
	_____	_____
	_____	_____
	_____	_____
Parents	_____	_____
	_____	_____
	_____	_____
	_____	_____
Students	_____	_____
	_____	_____
	_____	_____
	_____	_____

Larry J. Reynolds. *Successful Site-Based Management: A Practical Guide,* rev. ed. Copyright © 1997 by Corwin Press, Inc. Reprinted with permission.

WORKSHEET 18
Principal's Inventory of Special Programs and Projects

Identify the special programs and projects in your school that will compete with site-based management for the time, energy, and commitment of the school.

Program or Project	Persons Involved
1. New graduation requirements	
2. Outcomes-based education	
3. Accreditation process and demands	
4. Whole language	
5. Multicultural, gender-fair programs	
6. State-mandated programs	
7. Staff development	
8. Special funded projects	
9. Other	

Larry J. Reynolds. *Successful Site-Based Management: A Practical Guide*, rev. ed. Copyright © 1997 by Corwin Press, Inc. Reprinted with permission.

WORKSHEET 19
Principal's Inventory of School Decision-Making and Advisory Groups

For each of the special programs and projects listed in Worksheet 18, indicate the participation, if any, by members of the school in a related decision-making or advisory group. Also, list other advisory or decision-making groups that currently exist in the school. These groups may be either temporary or permanent committees and may involve students and parents as well as staff members.

Program or Project	Type of Group (Advisory or Decision Making)	Participants
1. _____	_____	_____
2. _____	_____	_____
3. _____	_____	_____
4. _____	_____	_____
5. _____	_____	_____
6. _____	_____	_____
7. _____	_____	_____
8. _____	_____	_____
9. _____	_____	_____

Larry J. Reynolds. *Successful Site-Based Management: A Practical Guide*, rev. ed. Copyright © 1997 by Corwin Press, Inc. Reprinted with permission.

The Principal: The Key to Success 73

WORKSHEET 20
Principal's Inventory of Activities and Use of Time

In the space below, estimate how you currently spend your time. Make up your own categories that make the most sense to you and that account for the majority of your time.

Type of Activity	Percentage of Time
1. _____	_____
2. _____	_____
3. _____	_____
4. _____	_____

Of the issues and problems facing the school that you identified in Worksheet 17, which ones require the most time on your part?

Issue or Problem

1. _____
2. _____
3. _____
4. _____

Of the special programs and projects that you identified in Worksheet 18, which ones require the most time on your part?

Special Program or Project

1. _____
2. _____
3. _____
4. _____

Larry J. Reynolds. *Successful Site-Based Management: A Practical Guide*, rev. ed. Copyright © 1997 by Corwin Press, Inc. Reprinted with permission.

In summary, the discussions and worksheets of this section have tried to describe the current issues and problems, special programs and projects, advisory and decision-making groups, and principal's activities and use of time in the individual school. The attempt has been to identify where the organization is putting its time and energy outside of the instructional routine of the school.

This analysis of the context of change is critical in determining how site-based management must be responsive to what already exists in the school. Site-based management, to be effective as a strategy for school improvement, will have to do the following:

- Address the current issues and problems
- Build on the current special projects and programs
- Define its role (i.e., the role of the site team) vis-à-vis the other existing decision-making and advisory groups

The goal of site-based management is to do more than manage the status quo: It is an overall strategy of school improvement. To meet this goal, the principal's leadership role is to move the school to the point where it can effectively use the strategic planning process, that is, shift its focus when necessary from specific issues and programs to a comprehensive picture of the school and its effectiveness.

The principal will need to play a leadership role in working with the site team to help the team build the perspectives and understandings necessary to accomplish the tasks listed above. The following sections focus on how the principal can fulfill this leadership role and lead the organization through a series of steps to increase its overall effectiveness.

Increasing Organizational Effectiveness

As a strategy for school improvement, site-based management has the potential to lead to school improvement in two interdependent areas: the quality of the instructional program and the quality of the work environment. These dual goals of site-based management are presented in Figure 6.1.

It is important for the principal to understand that the quality of the work environment will be the *first* concern of members of the organization. That is, school improvement will be defined by members of the organization first in terms of improving the immediate, concrete, day-to-day activities and experiences of the students, parents, and staff. For purposes here, improving the work environment

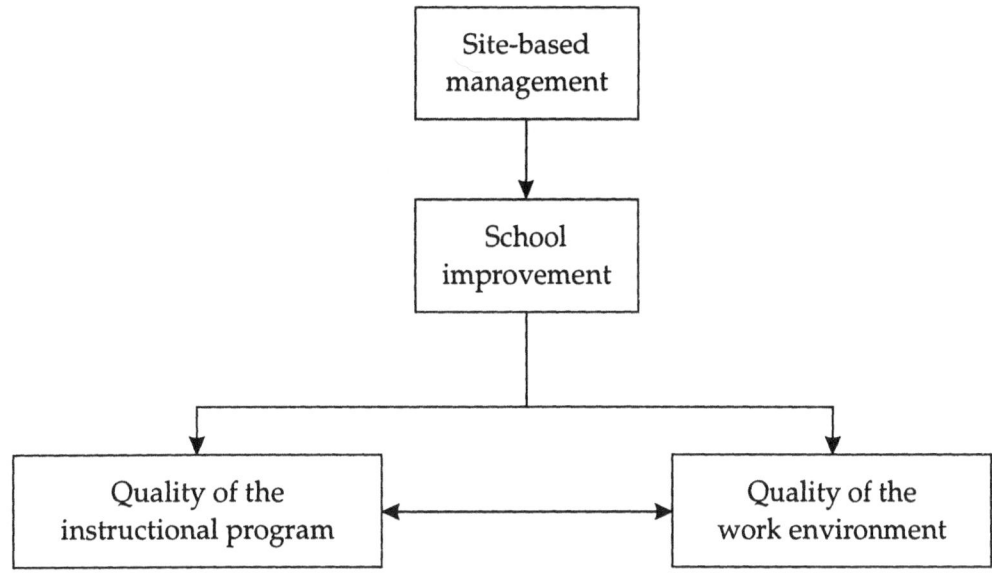

Figure 6.1. Goals of Site-Based Management

will be discussed in terms of two components: (a) meeting the management needs of the school and (b) creating a positive organizational climate. Only when the management needs of the organization and the organizational climate are perceived to be at a satisfactory level will the members of the school focus on the overall instructional program and long-range planning for the future.

To attain the goal of improving the quality of the instructional program and services of the school, the principal must lead the site team and staff to develop (a) positive attitudes and beliefs about change, (b) a schoolwide perspective of the educational program, and (c) an understanding and application of the strategic planning model for school improvement.

In summary, if the two goals are to be attained, then the task of the principal is to lead the organization through five successive steps to increase the effectiveness of the school. They are diagrammed in Figure 6.2.

Meeting the Management Needs of the School

As discussed in Chapter 2, teachers' priorities are tied to the classroom and the work conditions that either enhance or interfere with their instructional role. Until the work environment is perceived as satisfactory, the principal and the site team will find their time and attention necessarily drawn to this area of teacher needs (and indirectly parent and student needs).

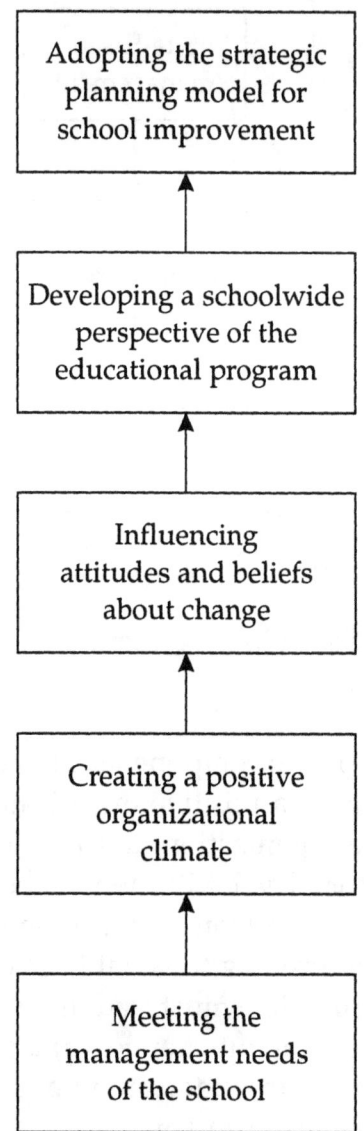

Figure 6.2. Increasing Organizational Effectiveness

The management needs of the work environment are presented in Table 6.1.

The unmet management needs of the school will demand constant attention and result in "brush-fire" management for the principal and, once formed, for the site team as well. The principal may want to refer to Worksheet 17 to identify which of the problems and issues of the school fall into this category. By referring to Worksheet 20, the principal can review the amount of time and energy that is spent on various management needs of the school.

Assistance from the central office on meeting management needs was proposed as a valuable *new role* of the central office. This new role is in contrast to

TABLE 6.1 Management Needs of Schools

Building maintenance	Budget	Special events
School calendar	Teacher evaluation	Special programs
Transportation	Tardiness	Staff development
Space needs	Purchasing	Hiring staff
Substitutes	Grading	Student teachers
Parent conferences	Supplies	Attendance
Business partnerships	Discipline	Staff meetings

traditional patterns of criticism or demands that the problems be solved. Indeed, the cause of the difficulty in some of these areas may well lie at the central office level and require attention in a number of buildings. Or the principal may want to appoint a temporary committee of teachers within the building to find ways to improve the current difficulty. Regardless of which approach the principal takes, the leadership role of the principal will have little or no credibility until the "real needs" of the staff are addressed.

These are the management needs of the school that the principal must satisfy to enable the site team and staff to devote effective time and attention to improving the instructional program of the school. If not, site-based management will only translate to "finding better ways to do the same thing."

Creating a Positive Organizational Climate

If school improvement is to reach beyond "finding better ways to do the same things," the principal will need to facilitate the creation of an organizational climate that is supportive of change efforts for improving the instructional program of the school.

Perhaps the greatest potential influence of the principal lies in his or her leadership in setting the organizational climate of the school. The organizational climate is what gives individual schools their distinct "personality." People intuitively understand the organizational climate even after spending a short period of time in a school building. Some schools feel warm and friendly; others are cold and formal. You feel welcome in some schools, like an intruder in others. Teachers and students seem relaxed in some schools, tense and guarded in others. In some schools teachers are positive and energetic; in others they are burned out and withdrawn. Whereas all schools in a given district may share common characteristics, strengths, and even problems, each school has its own climate.

This organizational climate is derived from a large number of subtle messages communicated by its members and the physical features of the building. It is "real" and it is easily identified by educators and others alike. It influences the activities and interactions of everyone in the school (students, parents, and staff), and it affects their levels of commitment, involvement, ownership, effectiveness, and satisfaction. It will also influence the process of site-based management.

The goals of site-based management are, in part, to increase the commitment, involvement, and ownership of organizational members and therefore increase their effectiveness and satisfaction. But site-based management will not attain these goals unless it exists in a daily organizational climate that also supports the attainment of these goals. A weekly meeting for a couple of hours will not be sufficient if the organizational climate itself serves to defeat the same goals. In fact, it is likely that the personality of the site team will reflect the current personality or organizational climate of the school.

The organizational climate will also influence, in part, how the staff views the need for change in the instructional program of the school. If the organizational climate is not positive and healthy, it will exhibit the following characteristics:

- A lack of trust: The motives and intentions of others are suspect; people are only looking out for themselves.
- Low risk taking: People believe that if you try something and it doesn't work, you'll get in trouble.
- Lack of respect for others: People believe that no one appreciates or understands what they do; why should they appreciate and understand what others do?
- Avoiding responsibility: People believe that they can't do their job because other people aren't doing theirs.
- No recognition for effort: People believe that nobody's going to know or recognize how hard they try.
- Closed communication: People believe that they never know what's going on until after somebody changes something.

A poor organizational climate exists when people are not respected for who they are, what they do, and their contribution to the overall effectiveness of the school. In this situation, people withdraw from others and retreat into their own world. They blame others when problems occur and find excuses for their own behavior when negatively judged by others. There is little confidence in the organization and in others to do the current job effectively, let alone tackle anything new.

TABLE 6.2 Organizational Climate Components

Trust in others	Recognition and rewards
Risk taking	Open communication
Respect for others	Continuous improvement
Accepting responsibility	High standards

If improvements in the instructional program of the school are to be made, a supportive organizational climate will have to be in place. An effective organizational climate is a function of the components listed in Table 6.2

The principal can again refer to Worksheet 17 to identify which of the problems and issues of the school fall under the category of organizational climate. And reference to Worksheet 20 will reveal the relative time the principal has been devoting to these issues.

The principal can best create a positive organizational climate by modeling the attitudes and behaviors expected of others. The specific techniques to do this are discussed in the following chapter, "Expanding the Role of the Principal."

Influencing Attitudes and Beliefs About Change

The third step the principal must take is to influence the attitudes and beliefs about educational change held by the staff. Although the staff may well agree that education, in general, needs to be improved and that things "could certainly be better around here," opinions will differ as to who needs to change and what needs to change.

Two basic orientations toward change, internal and external, can be identified (see Table 6.3). Whereas external changes are necessary to assist the schools in their mission, it is clear that as educators we have *greater* control over the internal system and internal changes. It is the role of the principal to help members of the organization realize where their scope of greatest influence lies and that they are not powerless to improve the status quo.

Developing a Schoolwide Perspective of the Educational Program

The principal is one of the few persons, and perhaps the only person, at the building level who is accustomed to taking a schoolwide perspective of the educational program. Education has evolved to the point where certification and job descriptions have generally created a system of specialization. And, as districts

TABLE 6.3 Basic Orientations Toward School Change

External Need for Change	Internal Need for Change
We are doing the best we can given what we have to work with.	We need to change both the "what" and "how" of teaching and learning.
We can do better by having more resources for more staff, smaller classes, better materials, and increased technology.	Although we need adequate resources, "more of the same" no longer equates with "better."
The needed changes are outside the system: more funding, better materials, increased parent involvement, and reduced crime and drugs.	The needed changes are inside the system: changes in priorities, better use of resources, restructuring, and greater flexibility and variability.

and schools increase in size, this specialization is reinforced. People's concerns are focused on their job. They describe themselves as a first-grade teacher or a high school English teacher. The curriculum work they do is in their own area, and their work-related interactions with other staff tend to be with those in the same department or at the same level.

Furthermore, a review and revision of the school program is typically broken down into subject areas. For example, "This year we will work on mathematics across the district and next year the cycle calls for us to look at art and music" or "We won't be adopting a new language arts program for another 2 years" or "The district is beginning a new gifted students program with its own teachers and students will be released from their regular classes to participate in this program."

As a result, in education we tend to focus on school effectiveness in terms of, first, our own performance and, second, our own particular grade level or subject area. Although the effectiveness of the overall school is of concern to us, it is not our primary interest because it has not been our responsibility.

In contrast, the approach advocated for site-based management is for all staff to focus on the total school program and its effectiveness. And the principal will have to provide the leadership in helping people to adopt this perspective.

Adopting the Strategic Planning Model for School Improvement

The fifth step the principal must take is to use the strategic planning model as a tool for the current program and school improvement efforts. Strategic planning is an activity that is frequently done by a committee and then filed away and, perhaps at best, is reviewed on a yearly basis. In our approach, the strategic plan

TABLE 6.4 Steps to Increase School Effectiveness

Improving the quality of the work environment	1. Meeting the management needs of the school
	2. Creating a positive organizational climate
Improving the quality of the instructional program	3. Influencing attitudes and beliefs about change
	4. Developing a schoolwide perspective of the educational program
	5. Adopting the strategic planning model for program improvement

is a working document. It provides a common language for the central office, the principal, the site team, and the school staff to use when talking about and making decisions about the instructional program of the school.

With greater building autonomy provided by site-based management, the staff will need to understand the big picture: not only how their individual role fits into the overall effort of the school but also how the school fits in with the overall strategic plan of the district. The effectiveness of the organization, at both the district level and the school level, is now coordinated by the strategic planning process.

Success will be achieved if the district and schools can answer yes to the following questions:

1. Are we being responsive to the external forces on the district and school?
2. Are we meeting the needs of the students?
3. Are our programs and operations consistent with our values and beliefs about education?
4. Are we using the vision as a reference for our decision making and school improvement?

Summary

If site-based management is to serve as a means to school improvement, then the principal's primary role is to help move the organization and staff through different levels of focus. The five levels of school effectiveness provide the schoolwide focus needed to attain both goals of site-based management—improvement in the quality of the work environment and in the quality of the instructional program. The steps for increasing school effectiveness are presented in Table 6.4.

As we discussed, meeting the management needs of the school will be the first priority of the staff. Attaining a satisfactory level will allow the principal to focus on increasingly comprehensive, schoolwide perspectives. Creating a positive organizational climate will facilitate site-based management providing participants with increased involvement, commitment, and ownership and leading to increased effectiveness and satisfaction. With a positive organizational climate, the principal can focus on influencing attitudes and beliefs about change by the staff and on potential internal changes to attain school improvement. With a schoolwide perspective, adopting the strategic planning model for program improvement will provide a common language and a comprehensive approach to school improvement linking both the district and individual building efforts.

In the next chapter, the actions that the principal can take to create a leadership role in site-based management and to facilitate the effectiveness of the site team will be presented.

7

Expanding the Role of the Principal

With the increased autonomy of site-based management comes greater responsibility for the school and for the principal. The impetus for school improvement in the district is now the responsibility of the individual schools. The principal's role can no longer be limited to managing the status quo (or even special projects and programs of the central office) through control and compliance. The principal must be a leader as well as a manager.[1]

As discussed in Chapter 6, the principal must meet both the management and leadership demands of the school by creating a school setting that improves the effectiveness of the school and supports site-based management.

The principal can build this setting by focusing on the following five steps:

1. Meeting the management needs of the school
2. Creating a positive organizational climate
3. Influencing attitudes and beliefs about change
4. Developing a schoolwide perspective of the educational program
5. Adopting the strategic planning model for school improvement

With the creation of this kind of school setting, teachers will be more effective as they express their expertise, creativity, and inventiveness and develop strategies that improve the quality of the instructional program.

Adopting Leadership Behaviors

There are no leaders without "followers." Leadership may or may not be attributed to an individual because of his or her formal position. Becoming a principal does not automatically make a person a leader even if it does make that person "the boss." Leadership is derived from others. As discussed in Chapter 2, followers expect leaders to demonstrate the following characteristics: vision, trust, credibility, and inspiration. These were defined in Table 2.2 on page 11. It is important to remember that these dimensions of leadership will be judged by others based on their daily activities and interactions with the principal. Therefore, if the principal wants to be seen as a leader, the "normal" and "routine" activities and interactions of the principal need to be consistent with the requirements of leadership even when the activities themselves may be of a management nature. As discussed below, management and leadership are distinct activities, but leadership is built on a foundation of credible management.

The extent to which the principal positively affects the school's effectiveness depends on the principal's ability to demonstrate vision, trust, credibility, and inspiration. In fact, this relationship is so strong that it is very difficult to have an effective school without an effective principal.

Just as there is a required sequence of steps to build the effectiveness of the organization and facilitate site-based management (see Chapter 6), there is a complementary sequence of steps in establishing the leadership role. Credibility is the first step, trust is the second step, and vision and inspiration are the last steps. It is hard to imagine that a principal can provide inspiration if credibility and trust do not exist.

The essential point is that the principal can build the leadership role through the same set of behaviors that will also increase the effectiveness of the organization. For example, the principal can establish credibility by meeting the management needs of the school. The sequence of steps in Table 7.1 shows the relationship between organizational effectiveness and the leadership behaviors of the principal.

The following sections will focus on the specific skills and behaviors that are required to meet the organization's needs for effectiveness and to establish the principal as a leader. The skills and behaviors of the principal necessary to establish leadership are different for each area of organizational effectiveness.

The discussion will address each area, following the suggested sequence of steps, and describe the skills and behaviors required.

Establishing Credibility

The principal's credibility can be established by meeting the management needs of the school. To do this, the principal must demonstrate technical expertise

Expanding the Role of the Principal

TABLE 7.1 Steps in Building the Leadership Role of the Principal

Sequence of Steps	Increasing Organizational Effectiveness	Building the Leadership Role
1	Meeting the management needs of the school	Establish credibility
2	Creating a positive organizational climate	Build trust
3	Developing positive attitudes and beliefs toward change	Provide vision and inspiration
	Developing a schoolwide perspective of the educational program	
	Adopting the strategic planning model for school improvement	

in each of the management areas of the school. That is, the principal must be perceived as capable of handling teacher supervision, parent conferences, budget preparation, hiring staff, student discipline, and so on. These are the real and most immediate needs of the staff. And this is why it has been suggested that the central office allocate resources to ensure that the school principals have the training, expertise, and assistance needed to meet these needs. In schools where there are assistant principals, responsibility may be delegated to others. But the principal is still responsible for these management areas, and any shortcomings in these areas will jeopardize the success of the principal's attempts to influence other areas of the school.

These demands are a constant in schools, and site-based management will not reduce the need for attention to be devoted to them. Indeed, they are so extensive in most schools that the majority of the principal's time and energy is primarily devoted to them to ensure that they are handled at a level that satisfies the parents, students, and staff.

It is important to note that there are many schools in which the perception is that site-based management has been developed to deal with management or administrative issues.[2] When this perception exists, teachers do not respond with enthusiasm toward site-based management. They are not typically interested in administration. In some settings, the site team deals with management issues by default because they are not handled in a satisfactory manner by the principal. Neither teacher interest nor satisfaction has been found to be very high in either of these circumstances. The effective management of the school is still the responsibility of the principal, and the time and energy of the site team can be better spent on school improvements that directly focus on the instructional program.

The principal's credibility will be enhanced if the staff is aware that the principal is striving toward continuous improvement in the management of the school. It is recommend that the staff be surveyed on a periodic basis to determine the current status or levels of satisfaction with each management area. Priorities and plans for improvement can then be formulated and communicated to the staff. Although the actual improvements must eventually be finalized, as long as the staff knows that problem areas are being worked on, the credibility of the principal is enhanced.

Worksheet 21 is presented as a guide in developing a survey that can be used by the principal with the school staff.

Because the focus in this book is the new role behaviors required of the principal under site-based management, technical skills are not discussed in further detail. It is difficult, however, to emphasize too strongly that the credibility of the principal as school manager is a necessary foundation for the leadership role.

Increasing Organizational Effectiveness	*Building the Leadership Role*	*Skills and Behaviors Required*
Meeting the management needs of the school	Establishing credibility	Technical skills
		Survey of current status of management needs

Developing Trust

The principal will not be able to influence the organizational climate of the school unless the members of the organization trust the principal. "Trust in others" is one of the components of a positive organizational climate (as presented in Table 6.2 on p. 79).

The behaviors of the principal that will promote trust are similar to several of the components essential for a positive organizational climate and are as follows:

- Treats others with courtesy and respect
- Shares credit and recognition
- Listens to others' opinions
- Accepts new ideas
- Shares information with others

WORKSHEET 21
Current Status of Management Needs

Indicate for each of the following areas those currently operating at a satisfactory level and those that need improvement. For those needing improvement, indicate how they could be improved.

Management Area	Satisfactory	Needs Improvement	Improve By
Building maintenance	_____	_____	_____
School calendar	_____	_____	_____
Transportation	_____	_____	_____
Space needs	_____	_____	_____
Substitutes	_____	_____	_____
Parent conferences	_____	_____	_____
Business partnerships	_____	_____	_____
Budget	_____	_____	_____
Teacher evaluation	_____	_____	_____
Tardiness	_____	_____	_____
Purchasing	_____	_____	_____
Grading	_____	_____	_____
Supplies	_____	_____	_____
Discipline	_____	_____	_____
Special events	_____	_____	_____
Special programs	_____	_____	_____
Staff development	_____	_____	_____
Hiring staff	_____	_____	_____
Student teachers	_____	_____	_____
Attendance	_____	_____	_____
Staff meetings	_____	_____	_____
Other	_____	_____	_____

Larry J. Reynolds. *Successful Site-Based Management: A Practical Guide*, rev. ed. Copyright © 1997 by Corwin Press, Inc. Reprinted with permission.

- Gives honest feedback
- Acts with integrity and high standards of ethics
- Makes decisions based on fact
- Accepts responsibility for own actions
- Admits mistakes
- States intentions and does what was said would be done

There are two strategies recommended for the principal to develop a relationship of trust with the members of the school and to create a positive organizational climate. The first of these is to interact regularly with all members of the organization. Trust is developed, in part, through interactions over time and as people get to know each other. The second strategy to build trust is to model the behaviors expected of others. The principal sets the tone of the organization. The norms and values that provide a positive organizational climate must be demonstrated by the principal's daily activities and interactions in the school. It is the most effective way to communicate what the principal values and what the principal's expectations are for others. These two areas are intertwined because as the interactions of the principal with other members of the organization increase, so do the opportunities to model the behaviors expected of others.

Interactions With Others

The greatest resource the principal has is his or her own time and attention. Whatever the principal attends to becomes important in the organization. If the principal emphasizes rules and regulations, then they will become important. If the principal emphasizes authority, then authority will become important. If the principal emphasizes people, then people will become important. It is the frequency of interactions and the nature of the relationships with others that will determine the trust people develop in the principal.

Being accessible is one way for the principal to increase the interactions with others. The daily routine of the school is rarely routine. Students, parents, and staff all have individual needs that require "immediate" attention. School buses are late, teachers are sick, the roof leaks, students are tardy, parents are concerned, supplies are needed, meetings are canceled, and no one knows where the overhead projector is. The principal, other building administrators, and office staff are all pressured to respond to these multiple and seemingly simultaneous demands.

Worksheet 22 is provided to assist the principal in thinking about his or her accessibility to others and the interactions that are initiated by other people. How is this pattern influencing your view of the school? Is it limiting your leadership opportunity?

Expanding the Role of the Principal 89

WORKSHEET 22
Accessibility Log for the Principal

Use the following form to keep track of the people who seek you out during the day.

Day	Person	Topic
___	_____	_____
___	_____	_____
___	_____	_____
___	_____	_____
___	_____	_____
___	_____	_____
___	_____	_____
___	_____	_____
___	_____	_____
___	_____	_____
___	_____	_____
___	_____	_____
___	_____	_____
___	_____	_____
___	_____	_____
___	_____	_____
___	_____	_____
___	_____	_____
___	_____	_____
___	_____	_____

What patterns emerge during the week? Is your accessibility to others following a pattern? If so, how is it influencing your view of the school? How is it limiting your leadership with the entire staff?

Larry J. Reynolds. *Successful Site-Based Management: A Practical Guide*, rev. ed. Copyright © 1997 by Corwin Press, Inc. Reprinted with permission.

It is important for the principal to do more than just be accessible to others in a reactive way. It is also important for the principal to set his or her own schedule of interactions. This will allow the principal to get a sampling of the total environment and to interact with others who are less likely to seek out the principal. Furthermore, trust is developed when people perceive the principal as knowledgeable about what is really going on in the school.

The principal can accomplish this by scheduling a part of each day to initiate interactions with others. It becomes a part of the principal's daily, scheduled activities, even though it need not, and should not, be at the same time each day. It is purposeful behavior scheduled to maximize the effect of the principal's leadership role. Some people refer to this type of activity as "management by walking around." This activity is critical for the leadership function as well and can be called "leading by walking around."

The principal can a create a simple matrix of individuals/groups/departments in the school and the days of the week. At the end of each day, the principal can check to see who was visited or talked with during the day. Those not talked with become the priority for the next day. The size of the school and the number of staff will dictate how often the principal can see everyone on an individual (or at least small, informal group) basis, but the goal is to interact with someone from each group on a daily basis. No one in the building should be missed; everyone should have equal importance during this "initiating behavior."

Assistant principals should also initiate interactions with the staff, but it should not be divided up by department or group. The common pattern is to divide management functions among the administrative staff: One person takes transportation, another scheduling, another parent conferences, and so on. This kind of activity is beyond the management function, and each member of the administrative team should participate. However, the principal must be involved actively in initiating interactions with the staff and should not assign this critical activity to another person.

Visiting classrooms on an informal basis is also a strategy that can enhance the principal's credibility and trust. The purpose of these visits should be clearly stated that it is *not* to evaluate or supervise teachers but to learn about how the program really works. The principal should ask to be invited into the classrooms. (Being invited will be a sign of trust.) These visits can provide the principal with further personal knowledge of the classroom program of the school, adding to the principal's credibility for knowing, at least to a greater extent, what it is really like in the classroom.

Worksheet 23 is provided to suggest how the principal can structure a daily schedule to "cover the school" in initiating interactions. It is followed by a blank form, Worksheet 24, for the principal's own use.

Expanding the Role of the Principal

WORKSHEET 23
Interactions Initiated by the Principal (Sample Form)

Use the following type of sheet to keep track of the interactions
you initiate while you are "leading by walking around."

Department/Grade Level/Team	M T W T F	Bus Drivers	M T W T F
Teacher	__ __ __ __ __	Driver 1	__ __ __ __ __
Teacher	__ __ __ __ __	Driver 2	__ __ __ __ __
Teacher	__ __ __ __ __	Driver 3	__ __ __ __ __
Department/Grade Level/Team	M T W T F	Volunteers	M T W T F
Teacher	__ __ __ __ __	Person 1	__ __ __ __ __
Teacher	__ __ __ __ __	Person 2	__ __ __ __ __
Teacher	__ __ __ __ __	Person 3	__ __ __ __ __
Specialists	M T W T F	Substitutes	M T W T F
Teacher	__ __ __ __ __	Teacher 1	__ __ __ __ __
Teacher	__ __ __ __ __	Teacher 2	__ __ __ __ __
Teacher	__ __ __ __ __	Teacher 3	__ __ __ __ __
Extracurricular Activities	M T W T F	Teacher Aides	M T W T F
Teacher	__ __ __ __ __	Person 1	__ __ __ __ __
Teacher	__ __ __ __ __	Person 2	__ __ __ __ __
Teacher	__ __ __ __ __	Person 3	__ __ __ __ __
Custodians	M T W T F	Office Staff	M T W T F
Person 1	__ __ __ __ __	Person 1	__ __ __ __ __
Person 2	__ __ __ __ __	Person 2	__ __ __ __ __

(continued on the next page)

Larry J. Reynolds. *Successful Site-Based Management: A Practical Guide*, rev. ed. Copyright © 1997 by Corwin Press, Inc. Reprinted with permission.

WORKSHEET 23
Continued

Cafeteria Staff	M	T	W	T	F	Other	M	T	W	T	F
Person 1	_	_	_	_	_	Person 1	_	_	_	_	_
Person 2	_	_	_	_	_	Person 2	_	_	_	_	_
Person 3	_	_	_	_	_	Person 3	_	_	_	_	_

Are there any persons or groups you are not seeing on a regular basis?

How is this influencing your view of the organization? Your leadership efforts?

Larry J. Reynolds. *Successful Site-Based Management: A Practical Guide,* rev. ed. Copyright © 1997 by Corwin Press, Inc. Reprinted with permission.

Modeling the Behaviors Expected of Others

Leadership by walking around provides the principal with the opportunity to model the behaviors expected of others in building a positive organizational climate.

The principal's personal interest and attention lets people know that what they are doing is important to the principal and the organization as well. It is a source of reward and recognition that can be positive, immediate, constant, visible to others, and valued. It sets the example of providing personal recognition from one person to another.

The principal's increased interactions provide an opportunity to demonstrate respect for others and an acceptance of all members of the organization. The existence or perception of an "elite" in the school will be diminished considerably by the principal's ignoring such distinctions and valuing the potential and contributions of all members of the organization.

The principal can encourage continuous improvement and risk taking by personally accepting new ideas and trying new approaches. The principal can communicate support to other staff by his or her personal interest and recognition of their efforts. By withholding judgments until new practices have had sufficient time to reveal their strengths and weaknesses, the principal can build trust by making decisions based on fact rather than personal preferences.

WORKSHEET 24
Interactions Initiated by the Principal

Use the following sheet to keep track of the interactions
you initiate while you are "leading by walking around."

Group/Department/Team	M	T	W	T	F	Group/Department/Team	M	T	W	T	F
_____	_	_	_	_	_	_____	_	_	_	_	_
_____	_	_	_	_	_	_____	_	_	_	_	_
_____	_	_	_	_	_	_____	_	_	_	_	_
_____	_	_	_	_	_	_____	_	_	_	_	_
_____	_	_	_	_	_	_____	_	_	_	_	_
_____	_	_	_	_	_	_____	_	_	_	_	_
_____	_	_	_	_	_	_____	_	_	_	_	_
_____	_	_	_	_	_	_____	_	_	_	_	_
_____	_	_	_	_	_	_____	_	_	_	_	_
_____	_	_	_	_	_	_____	_	_	_	_	_
_____	_	_	_	_	_	_____	_	_	_	_	_
_____	_	_	_	_	_	_____	_	_	_	_	_
_____	_	_	_	_	_	_____	_	_	_	_	_
_____	_	_	_	_	_	_____	_	_	_	_	_
_____	_	_	_	_	_	_____	_	_	_	_	_
_____	_	_	_	_	_	_____	_	_	_	_	_

Are there any persons or groups you are not seeing on a regular basis?

How is this influencing your view of the organization? Your leadership efforts?

Larry J. Reynolds. *Successful Site-Based Management: A Practical Guide*, rev. ed. Copyright © 1997 by Corwin Press, Inc. Reprinted with permission.

The accessibility and increased interaction of the principal can facilitate open communication in the organization through the increased sharing of information with others and by increasing the opportunity for more immediate feedback.

If the principal sets high standards for his or her own behavior, the principal will have increased credibility in communicating high standards for others. He or she can help other staff members set high standards for their own behavior by being aware of their goals and supportive of their efforts. The principal can assure people that what they do is important by merely giving it his or her own time and attention.

And finally, the principal can demonstrate accepting responsibility rather than blaming others or making excuses. By admitting and correcting mistakes, the principal allows the organization to "move on." And, through increased interaction with others, the principal is able to set the future directions.

There is a great variety of instruments available that can be used by the principal to assess his or her own personal style and the organizational climate of the school. These may be of considerable assistance to the principal and, ultimately, to the site team as well. It is beyond the scope of this book to extensively review or discuss them.

However, Worksheet 25 will allow the principal to briefly view his or her perceptions of the principal's behavior and level of trust in the organization. In addition, Worksheet 26 provides a quick rating scale of the organizational climate of the school and the extent to which the principal models the behaviors for a positive organizational climate.

In summary, the actions the principal must take to build trust and create a positive organizational climate go hand-in-hand. The skills and behaviors required of the principal in addressing this area of organizational effectiveness are as follows:

Increasing Organizational Effectiveness	*Building the Leadership Role*	*Skills and Behaviors Required*
Creating a positive organizational climate	Building trust	Interpersonal skills
		Increasing interactions
		Modeling the behaviors expected of others
		Self-assessment of trust
		Assessment of organizational climate

Expanding the Role of the Principal 95

WORKSHEET 25
Principal's Self-Assessment of Trust

Rate yourself on the following dimensions of trust in terms of the extent to which you believe you exhibit the following behaviors when interacting with others.

Behaviors Promoting Trust	(low) 1	2	3	4	(high) 5
Treats others with courtesy and respect	—	—	—	—	—
Shares credit and recognition	—	—	—	—	—
Listens to others' opinions	—	—	—	—	—
Accepts new ideas	—	—	—	—	—
Shares information with others	—	—	—	—	—
Gives honest feedback	—	—	—	—	—
Acts with integrity and high standards of ethics	—	—	—	—	—
Makes decisions based on fact	—	—	—	—	—
Accepts responsibility for own actions	—	—	—	—	—
Admits mistakes	—	—	—	—	—
States intentions and does what was said would be done	—	—	—	—	—

Which areas represent your greatest strengths?
How do these benefit the organization?

Which areas are in need of improvement?
How will improvements benefit the organization?

Larry J. Reynolds. *Successful Site-Based Management: A Practical Guide*, rev. ed. Copyright © 1997 by Corwin Press, Inc. Reprinted with permission.

WORKSHEET 26
Principal's Assessment of Organizational Climate

Indicate your perceptions of your own behavior and of the overall organization.

Components of a Positive Organizational Climate	Rating for Principal's Behaviors (low) 1 2 3 4 5 (high)	Rating for Organization as a Whole (low) 1 2 3 4 5 (high)
Trust in others	— — — — —	— — — — —
Risk taking	— — — — —	— — — — —
Respect for others	— — — — —	— — — — —
Accepting responsibility	— — — — —	— — — — —
Recognition and rewards	— — — — —	— — — — —
Open communication	— — — — —	— — — — —
Continuous improvement	— — — — —	— — — — —
High standards	— — — — —	— — — — —

What patterns emerge? Which areas do you need to improve on?

What patterns do you see in the organization?
What does this suggest for your leadership efforts in the future?

Larry J. Reynolds. *Successful Site-Based Management: A Practical Guide,* rev. ed. Copyright © 1997 by Corwin Press, Inc. Reprinted with permission.

Vision and Inspiration

The third and fourth leadership areas of the principal are vision and inspiration. If the management needs of the school are being met and a positive organizational climate exists, then the principal can realistically focus on instructional improvements. The task of the principal now becomes that of

- Creating a positive attitude toward change by members of the organization
- Developing a schoolwide perspective of the educational program by the members of the organization
- Adopting the strategic planning model for school improvement

The principal can use site-based management as a catalyst for school improvement in the building. Working with the site team will be the key. However, it will take time for the site team to get organized and begin to build on the districtwide vision and strategic plan. In the early stages, the principal can begin to create the attitudes and perspectives that will facilitate the initial work of the site team. And, after the site team becomes productive, the principal will need to maintain the same behaviors to reinforce the legitimacy and effectiveness of the site team.

The increased level of interaction of the principal with members of the organization not only helps to create a positive organizational climate but also provides the opportunity for a new focus on the instructional program. The leadership behaviors of the principal that will facilitate this new focus are as follows:

- Refers to the vision and strategic plan in everyday discussions about the instructional program
- Demonstrates a customer focus in interactions with parents and students
- Asks the right questions to encourage continual improvement
- Is an active learner about new instructional programs and strategies
- Acts as a catalyst in suggesting new programs and strategies
- Uses positive language when talking about others and the future
- Displays confidence in self and others
- Demonstrates energy in all activities

The strategic plan and vision of the district will be implemented through the building-level visions and strategic plans. Unfortunately, most strategic plans are never really used. After intensive work involving a large number of people over a long period of time, strategic plans and visions are frequently filed and forgotten. They are perceived as too long range and idealistic. They need to be perceived as a guide to action for all individuals in the organization.

The principal can set the guide-to-action precedent by personally using the vision as "the common language" about the instructional program. Using the new language allows central office and building staff; teachers and parents; and teachers of different subjects, grade levels, and specialties to understand each other when they talk about goals, activities, and results. It helps develop the necessary schoolwide perspective by avoiding the narrow focus on the specifics of any one program or activity.

Each principal, then, will need to become an expert on the districtwide strategic plan and vision and, specifically, how it applies to his or her particular setting. The principal will then help the site team and staff use the broader perspective as they generate the school's own, more specific strategic plan and vision.

Using the vision and strategic planning process will facilitate a customer focus in the school and encourage asking the right questions. What are the needs of our students and parents? How can we improve our existing programs and services? What programs and services are needed additions to what we are doing now? How will this decision affect our students and parents? How can our programs and services be better coordinated in the school? With others in the district? With others in the community?

The principal will help others develop a positive attitude toward change by being an active learner about new programs that might be appropriate for the school. Rather than waiting for teachers to suggest new strategies, the principal must act as a catalyst by learning about new standards, practices, and materials and suggesting them to the staff as possibilities. And, by asking the staff for their opinions, the principal recognizes their expertise, facilitates their involvement, and rewards their initiative.

The inspiration provided by the principal must come in part from an optimism about the future that is reflected in the positive language, confidence, and energy of the principal. Exhibiting this attitude and a personal style will draw out the same in others, building a new level of energy that releases the staff's full resources, increases the staff's effectiveness, and therefore, improves the effectiveness of the school as a whole.

Increasing Organizational Effectiveness	Building the Leadership Role	Skills and Behaviors Required
Creating a positive attitude toward change	Providing vision and inspiration	Use the vision and strategic plan
		Demonstrate a customer focus
Developing a schoolwide perspective		Ask the right questions
Adopting the strategic planning model		Be an active learner
		Act as a catalyst
		Use positive language
		Display confidence
		Demonstrate energy

Summary of Leadership Requirements for the Principal

Table 7.2 summarizes the skills and behaviors the principal can use to build his or her leadership role in the school and, at the same time, increase the organizational effectiveness of the school.

Defining New Roles and Accountability

Adopting new roles and responsibilities is the final step for the principal in the process of implementing site-based management. Thus far, the emphasis has been on the role changes necessary for the principal to assume an active leadership role in the school. It is also critical to establish clarity about the lines of authority—who is responsible to whom and for what. As explained in Chapter 5, the site team has the authority to make decisions with regard to budget, staffing, and program within the parameters established by the district. The principal has the responsibility for the overall effectiveness of the school, with the school staff remaining directly responsible to the principal. The principal, however, is responsible to the site team and the central office for *implementing* the decisions of the site team and *supervising* the staff's performance in a manner that is consistent with the shared vision of the school.

TABLE 7.2 Skills and Behaviors Required of the Principal

Sequence of Steps	Increasing Organizational Effectiveness	Building the Leadership Role	Skills and Behaviors Required
1	Meeting the management needs of the school	Establish credibility	Technical skills Survey of current status of management needs
2	Creating a positive organizational climate	Build trust	Interpersonal skills Increasing interactions Modeling the behaviors expected of others Self-assessment of trust Assessment of organizational climate
3	Developing positive attitudes and beliefs toward change Developing a schoolwide perspective of the educational program Adopting the strategic planning model for school improvement	Provide vision and inspiration	Use the vision and strategic plan Demonstrate a customer focus Ask the right questions Be an active learner Act as a catalyst Use positive language Display confidence Demonstrate energy

Important authority distinctions emerge:

1. The site team is a decision-making body, not a supervisory one.
2. The principal supervises all staff.
3. The principal is not free to veto the decisions of the site team.
4. The district retains formal authority over both the site team and the principal.
5. The district vision and strategic plan guide the activities of the site team.

The effectiveness of the organization and the success of site-based management, however, requires more than formal roles and lines of authority. Shared

Expanding the Role of the Principal

responsibility and effective leadership from all three groups—the central office, the principal, and the site team—is required.

For example, the principal will need to take the leadership in explaining his or her role in increasing the organizational effectiveness of the school using the model as presented in this chapter:

1. Meeting the management needs of the school
2. Building a positive organizational climate
3. Creating a positive attitude toward change
4. Developing a schoolwide perspective
5. Adopting the strategic planning model

The principal's accountability includes sharing three types of information that will be helpful to both the central office and to the site team during the implementation of site-based management.

1. The principal's assessment of the context of change (Worksheets 17, 18, and 19)
2. The current status of management needs (Worksheet 21)
3. The principal's assessment of the organizational climate (Worksheet 26)

It is important to note that these assessments are produced from the principal's perspective. They are not formal surveys of the staff or the parents and the community. The site team may wish to use surveys as part of its strategic planning in the future, but the team members will need to get organized and develop as a group before they can effectively begin the strategic planning process. The information from the principal's assessments, however, will provide helpful initial information to the site team in its "getting organized" activities (see Chapter 8).

This information is part of the ongoing communication required among the central office, the principal, and the site team to define the context of change for site-based management. The principal's assessments allow the central office to understand the conditions under which site-based management is being introduced and to provide resources to the principals to facilitate their effectiveness. And the assessments allow the principal to focus on the organizational development work that is necessary to "pave the way" for site-based management.

Furthermore, the principal should act as a link between the central office and the site team in bringing the resources of the central office to assist in the implementation of site-based management in the following areas:

- Shared visions
- Paperwork and compliance
- Personal growth and development

- Promising practices
- Problem solving
- Information and communication
- Human environments

And finally, the principal must be sensitive to the existing special programs and projects and existing advisory and decision-making groups in the school. These groups will be concerned about their status in the future and how their influence and power will be affected by site-based management and the site team. There will be a transition period while the site team is formed and begins its own group development activities. It is essential that the principal communicates that these groups need not disband because of site-based management but that they, like everyone else, will be influenced by the overall strategic planning and shared vision in the future.

In summary, the principal is the key to the successful implementation of site-based management. The role of the principal is more complex under site-based management, and the process of implementation requires new knowledge and skills, new belief systems, and new patterns of interaction. As presented in the past two chapters, the five steps for the principal are as follows:

1. Adopt a systemwide perspective.
2. Assess the context of change.
3. Implement an effectiveness plan to facilitate site-based management.
4. Adopt leadership behaviors.
5. Define new roles and accountability.

By completing these steps, the principal can build on the work at the district level and lead the site team to success in identifying and implementing school improvements.

Notes

1. *The Leadership Challenge* (1987) by Kouzes and Posner is an interesting and highly informative book on the many aspects of behavior that individuals can adopt to enhance their leadership role. The distinction between leaders and managers is one of many valuable leadership topics discussed by Bennis and Nanus in their book *Leaders* (1985).

2. In *School-Based Reform: Taking Stock*, Murphy and Beck (1995) state that site-based management in most settings has a "misdirected focus." They found that site-based management increased the time and attention to administrative and management issues rather than to instructional issues and school improvement.

8

Structuring the Site Team for Success

The site team at the building level can be formed now that the central office and principals have done their work. The new roles and activities of both the central office and the principal have been designed to enhance the potential success of the site team, that is, to increase (a) the quality of decisions about the instructional program and services of the school, (b) the effectiveness of these programs and services, and (c) ultimately, student success.

The intention from the beginning has been to structure site-based management so that it brings about a significant change from the status quo by making the site team responsible for significant decisions at the school level. To this end, the following has been accomplished.

First, the central office has created a strategic plan for the district by the following:

- Identifying the external forces acting on the district
- Defining the current and future needs of students
- Clarifying the values and beliefs about education
- Developing a shared vision of the future
- Defining the expectations and parameters for schools
- Identifying the management needs of schools
- Creating support roles for leadership and service

Second, the expectations for the expanded role of the principal have been defined as follows:

- Meeting the leadership and management needs of the school by increasing the organizational effectiveness of the school and building an organizational context that will facilitate the success of site-based management.
- Producing the outputs required to help both the central office and the site team understand the factors that will influence the functioning and success of site-based management in the specific school setting. The outputs are an assessment of the context of change, an assessment of the management needs of the school, and an assessment of the organizational climate of the school.

Third, the authority relationships have been established among the central office, the principal, and the site team. These are summarized as follows:

- The site team is responsible to the central office for strategic planning at the building level, the development of a shared vision at the building level, and the development and evaluation of school improvement plans at the building level. Its duties are analysis, problem solving, priority setting, and planning. It makes decisions in the areas of budget, staffing, and programs and services within the parameters and expectations established by the central office.
- The principal is responsible for providing leadership and technical assistance to the site team, creating an organizational context supportive of site-based management, supervising the implementation of the school improvement priorities and plans of the site team, and managing the day-to-day operations of the school.
- The district is responsible for its strategic planning and outputs to provide overall direction to the district schools and to facilitate the work and success of both the principal and the site team.

All the above have been designed to enhance the satisfaction and productivity of the members of the site team. As research has shown (Robbins, 1993, p. 314), group productivity and satisfaction are likely to be enhanced when the following conditions have been met:

1. Members are required to use a variety of relatively high-level skills.
2. The group task is a whole and meaningful piece of work with a visible outcome.
3. The outcomes of the group's work on the task have significant consequences for other people either inside or outside the organization.

TABLE 8.1 Strengths and Weaknesses of Group Decision Making

Strengths	Weaknesses
More complete information and knowledge	Time consuming
Increased diversity of views	Pressures to conform
Increased acceptance of a solution	Domination by a few members
Increased legitimacy	Ambiguous responsibility

4. The task provides group members with substantial autonomy for deciding about how they do the work.

5. Work on the task generates regular, trustworthy feedback about how well the group is performing.

Although factors external to the group are an important influence on its levels of productivity and satisfaction, the nature of the group itself will also be a critical source of influence. In the following section, a number of factors are identified that are believed to be critical in the site team's first step in implementing site-based management.

Getting Started

Group decision making has a number of potential strengths and weaknesses (Robbins, 1993, pp. 346-347). The key in building the structure and membership of the group is to try to maximize the group's strengths and minimize its weaknesses. The strengths and weaknesses of groups in decision making are listed in Table 8.1

The first step for the building is to determine how the site team is to be structured and who will serve on the team. In some situations, a planning committee is selected to plan how to set up the site team. In others, the principal is given the authority by the central office to create the site council. Whatever the strategy selected by the central office or the principal, it is strongly suggested that a representative group is involved in this first step.

The credibility of the site team and the initial levels of trust the school community has in the group will be a function of how the group is initially selected. And the principal's role in this process will also be critical, sending a clear signal about the principal's attitude toward site-based management and how sincere the principal is about sharing responsibility and power. In general, the wider the representation of the staff, parents, and community in organizing the team, the more likely the site team will be perceived as a potentially important and viable group in the school.

Sometimes existing committees are selected to serve in an expanded capacity as the site team, for example, an existing school improvement team or a staff council. If this option is considered, the following questions need to be asked. Is the membership of the existing group consistent with the representation desired on the site team? Can the existing group shift to a new set of responsibilities? Will the group's previous responsibilities interfere with new ones? What is the current level of performance and satisfaction of the group? What are the levels of credibility and trust of the committee as perceived by others?

Whatever approach is taken to create the new site team, the first task is to define the following elements. They should be communicated to establish clearly the external framework within which the site team will function. (These can be listed on Worksheet 27.)

1. Definition of the purpose of the site team
2. Description of its authority in decision making
3. Description of the steps the team is to follow in implementing site-based management
4. List of the criteria by which school effectiveness will be judged by the central office
5. List of the expectations for site-based management of the central office
6. List of the specific decision areas delegated to the site team by the central office
7. List of the continuing districtwide programs in the school
8. Definition of the current decision-making responsibilities of other advisory and decision-making groups in the school

The second task is to focus on the initial structure and membership of the site team. The following considerations are important to provide prospective members with a clear sense of who else will serve on the site team and the expectations for participation.

Group Size

The size of decision-making groups has a direct influence on the ability to maximize strengths and minimize weaknesses. Generally, the larger the group, the more diverse the information and knowledge of the group. And larger groups

Structuring the Site Team for Success

WORKSHEET 27
Defining the Role of the Site Team

Complete the definitions for each of the following areas.

Role-Defining Area	Definition or Description
1. Purpose	
2. Authority	
3. Steps in implementation	
4. Criteria by which school effectiveness is to be judged by the central office	
5. Expectations for site-based management held by the central office	
6. Decision-making areas included in budget, staffing, and program	
7. Continuing districtwide projects and programs	
8. Other advisory and decision-making groups	

Larry J. Reynolds. *Successful Site-Based Management: A Practical Guide*, rev. ed. Copyright © 1997 by Corwin Press, Inc. Reprinted with permission.

tend to be more creative than smaller groups. However, the larger the group, the more inefficient it becomes. Furthermore, as groups increase in size, there is a greater tendency for them to be dominated by a few individuals.

Educators are frequently tempted to increase the size of the group beyond that which is needed. When participation and a sense of ownership is the goal, schools frequently try to include representatives from every possible stakeholder group in public education. Some schools follow the rule that if one representative of a group is good, then two will be twice as good. The "democratic" rationale for site-based management suggests that no one should be left out.

To avoid the group size problem, it helps to have your goals for site-based management clear. Because the duties of site teams are centered on accomplishing the tasks of strategic planning, creating a shared vision, and developing program improvement plans, we believe a smaller group is preferable. It is suggested that the group number no more than 8 to 10 members. By including the principal, staff members, and parents (and students at the secondary level), the site team can very quickly reach 10 members. It is important to remember that the site team can, and it is argued must, seek out the participation and involvement of all the members of the organization if it is to assume an effective leadership role. Involvement in key issues should not be limited to membership on the site team. The site team will have the opportunity to form ad hoc committees on specific priorities that should be opened to wider participation.

A second reason for limiting the size of the group is the sheer number of committees that exist in most schools today. Teachers frequently find themselves, by choice or requirement, to be members of a variety of committees, each with its own time demands.

Another reason for limiting the size of the group is the time commitment necessary to make the site team function effectively. For this reason, it is recommended that teachers receive released time or additional compensation as members of the site team. This arrangement will help to establish the importance and legitimacy of the site team. If it is to be considered part of a teacher's legitimate role, then the teaching load should be reduced because of the additional responsibility. If the teacher is acting in a capacity beyond that which is defined as the teaching role, then the teacher should receive extra compensation (as do coaches of athletic teams). The larger the size of the group, however, the greater the number of teachers on the team and the less feasible this option becomes.

The final reason for a smaller group is simply to start slowly. It is easier to schedule meetings and build positive working relationship when there are fewer people involved. The focus of the site team must be its own success in the early stages of group development.

Group Diversity

One of the potential strengths of group decision making is the availability of a diversity of perceptions, knowledge, and skills of group members. Because the site team is responsible for strategic planning, a shared vision of the future, and the effectiveness of educational programs and services for all students of the school, it is critical that the site team reflect the diversity of the school community of parents, students, and staff. The credibility and legitimacy of site-based management depend on it.

Criteria for Selecting Members

The specific school setting will determine many of the criteria for group membership. The history of the school, its issues and problems, the previous levels of involvement in advisory and decision-making groups, and the past influence and power of individuals and groups are all important considerations. However, there are three additional criteria that should be included with those above. These three are consistent with the goals and process described thus far.

First, members of the group should be selected for their potential to assume a leadership role. The intended role of the site team is leadership, and if they are to assume that collective role, then the members must be able to exhibit the characteristics of leaders. These were discussed in the chapters on the principal. The characteristics of vision, credibility, trust, and inspiration can be inferred from the past behavior of individuals considered for membership. It is not necessary that they have held a formal leadership position in the past, only that they have the potential to be perceived by others as having these characteristics.

Second, the potential members should have the interest and ability to adopt a schoolwide focus, that is, a big-picture view of issues and considerations for school improvement. It is recommended that people with a single-issue focus be avoided whether they are parents, staff, or students. This does not mean that different members should not have any priorities or interests, but it does mean that they have the flexibility to look at issues that are important to other people as well.

Third, the potential members should demonstrate an interest and concern for all the students in the school. The success of the site team and the effectiveness of the instructional program and services of the school depend on the ability for all students to maximize their success. It is selecting members who simply like the students and enjoy spending time with them. These people demonstrate their concern by their daily interactions and activities with students and by how they talk about students to others. It is imperative that the site team be student centered rather than adult centered and reinforces the "students as the customer" orientation.

Different Status of Members

One of the characteristics that will determine the group's productivity and the satisfaction of each member is the formal status of different members. If the site team reflects the traditional hierarchy of formal roles in the organization, then the team is likely to reinforce the old patterns and be dominated by those individuals with the highest formal status. This can interfere with the ability of site-based management to emerge as a significant change in the decision-making structure and process of the district and the individual school. This may occur in several ways.

First, the principal's formal position "over" teachers and staff members and a principal's desire for continued control and compliance may result in efforts to dominate the group. This is one reason it is strongly suggested that the principal does not serve as chair of the group. In fact, the principal's leadership and facilitating role can be more effective without the responsibility of running the meeting.

Second, some schools believe in site-based management but are not enthusiastic about parents and community members participating as members of the site team. Educators frequently reinforce noninvolvement of parents by resorting to a "we are the experts" approach to discussions about students and educational programs and services. Parents often feel that their participation is not really wanted and their potential contributions not valued. Therefore, care is needed in establishing their role so they can participate fully.

Third, students frequently have the least power and influence in the school when it comes to identifying priorities for school improvement. At the same time, educators are concerned that students do not seem to want to assume more responsibility. We are increasingly interested in students learning leadership skills, problem-solving skills, and higher-order thinking skills. The membership of students on the site team and how that participation is received by the other adult members will demonstrate the true sensitivity of the site team about the interests and concerns of students and the extent to which the school is student centered.

Fourth, in some districts, school board members have also become members of the site team. It is strongly urged that this dual membership in the decision-making levels of the organization be avoided. School board members have a very different role and function to serve in a districtwide capacity. As members of an individual site team, the perspective is site centered. It is very difficult to manage two perspectives simultaneously. Furthermore, it is likely that the time demands of each position will prohibit effective service to either. And, in several instances, school board members on site teams have served only to reinforce the traditional structure and management role of control and compliance at higher levels of the organization and eroded the trust and credibility of site-based management from the beginning.

Structuring the Site Team for Success 111

As members of the site team are selected, by the principal or special committee, the different and previous status of the members will need to be considered as a factor that will influence the group in the future.

Group Norms

It is important to create a set of norms for the site team that will be the initial expectations for the participation of the group's members. These initial expectations can address such issues as the different statuses of group members and recognize the potential contribution of each person and the group he or she represents. In general, however, the group norms should be a preliminary statement of how the group is expected to work together. Once the actual team is formed, this early statement should be refined.

Essentially, the group norms for each individual's participation should be similar to those behaviors of the principal that are necessary to develop trust. These were discussed in Chapter 7 (see p. 86). There may be additional norms for the group that are particularly appropriate given the school setting and its history of issues and personalities. These should be identified and stated from the very beginning.

Work Setting

The last area to specify during the formation of the site team is the time, location, and frequency of the site-team meetings. It is important to give prospective members some initial sense of the time and travel commitments involved in membership.

Summary

Worksheet 28 is provided for the use of the planning group to define the structure and membership of the site team.

It is now possible, with the completion of Worksheets 27 and 28, for the planning group to select the members of the site team. By giving serious consideration to the role of the site team, its structure, and the selection process, it is possible to take into account the factors that contribute to both the strengths and weaknesses of group decision making.

It will be important for the planning group to keep the school community clearly informed. Members may be either appointed by a planning committee, the principal, or existing groups, or they may be elected by the staff and other existing organizations such as the parents association. It will be critical, however, to communicate

WORKSHEET 28
Defining the Structure and Membership of the Site Team

For each category, indicate the decision or solution and the supporting rationale.

Category	Decision or Solution	Rationale
Group size		
Group diversity		
Criteria for selecting members		
Different status of members		
Group norms		
Work setting		

Larry J. Reynolds. *Successful Site-Based Management: A Practical Guide*, rev. ed. Copyright © 1997 by Corwin Press, Inc. Reprinted with permission.

clearly the purpose of the site team and the criteria for membership to keep the selection process an open one. If not, the credibility of the site team will suffer.

Initial Activities

Once the site team is formed, it will be important for the group to complete a number of initial activities to get its collective feet on the ground. Frequently, the principal has been given the responsibility for starting the site team. If this is the case, the principal may want to lead the new team through the first five activities. Or a facilitator from the central office may want to lead the group's initial activities. It is suggested that the site team delay selecting a permanent chair until the group members begin to know each other better and the group itself has clarified its norms for working together. The initial activities are as follows:

1. Getting to know each other
2. Defining internal and external communication needs
3. Reviewing and revising group norms
4. Reviewing external influences on the team
5. Understanding the context of change
6. Selecting members for leadership positions
7. Reviewing the yearly cycle of the school

Getting to Know Each Other

The extent to which the new members know each other will vary from site team to site team. In smaller schools, it may be that everyone has known each other for years. In larger schools, this will probably be less likely. Although the principal and staff members may know each other well, parents and members from the general community will not know each other or the principal and the staff nearly as well.

The first activity of the group, then, should be to facilitate an increased knowledge of each other. This can be accomplished by a number of introductory or warm-up activities that allow group members to get to know each other as individuals. These activities include sharing personal information about background, interests, and summary information about their families. Often, longer breaks are scheduled during the first several meeting so members can engage in informal conversations to build greater familiarity with each other.

It is critical, however, that the group move beyond a knowledge of common interests and backgrounds *before* it begins the business of the group. It will be especially important for the educators to make the noneducators feel welcome and valued. Some of the early questions that new members of *any* group ask themselves are, Will I be accepted? Who else is here? and What role can I play? These questions may be especially pertinent when educators and noneducators begin to interact in shared decision-making setting.

The activities in Worksheet 29 are designed to help with this early, forming stage of the group and help the individuals to begin to become a team with a shared vision.

Structuring the Site Team for Success

WORKSHEET 29
Getting to Know Each Other

Activity 1: Why are you here?

Have each person in the group spend 2-3 minutes thinking about why he or she decided to become a member of the site team. Then have each member share the reason(s) with the total group. Select a group member to record them on large sheets. Save and give typed copies to all members at the next meeting.

Activity 2: What do you bring to the group?

Have each person in the group spend 2-3 minutes thinking about the contributions he or she can make to the group. The contribution may be based on experience, knowledge, skills, perspectives, ideas, commitment, people skills, and so on. Have each member share the potential contribution with the entire group. Record answers on large sheets. Save and give typed copies to all members at the next meeting.

Activity 3: Vision of future success

Congratulations! After just 1 year, your site team has been selected as the most effective site team in the state. Your school and team is to receive an award for excellence and you have been chosen to accept the award. You have been asked to say a few words describing what has made your site team so productive and so satisfying. What do you say (besides thank you)?

Give all the members 5 minutes to compose their acceptance speeches. Then have each member share his or her reason for the team's success. Record and give typed copies to all members at the next meeting.

Larry J. Reynolds. *Successful Site-Based Management: A Practical Guide*, rev. ed. Copyright © 1997 by Corwin Press, Inc. Reprinted with permission.

Defining Communication Needs

The newly formed site team needs to set an immediate precedent of clear, consistent, and timely communication with its members and with the school community. The basic rule for the site team (as it was for the district in beginning site-based management) is to "communicate even when you don't think you have anything to say."

It will be important to meet the internal communication needs of the group by preparing agendas prior to each meeting and distributing minutes of each meeting as soon as possible after the meeting. And, of course, good communication during the meeting is critical and will be discussed under Reviewing and Revising Group Norms below.

The external communication needs of the group, in the early stages, will be to explain to others what the site team is doing and why. If the site team fails to so inform the school community, different individuals may begin to assume, or suspect, that the site team is being withdrawn, or secretive, for any number of reasons.

It will be helpful for the group to spend 15 to 20 minutes at the first meeting talking about what others will want to know about the site team. Worksheet 30 is designed to assist in defining the internal and external communication strategies.

Structuring the Site Team for Success

WORKSHEET 30
Meeting Communication Needs

Activity 1: Internal communication needs

Have the group brainstorm answers to the following questions and select the strategies that best meet the needs of the site team.

1. What do we need to know before each meeting?
2. What do we need to record from each meeting?
3. How will we produce and distribute our agendas and minutes to the group?

Activity 2: External communication needs

Have the group brainstorm answers to the following questions and select the strategies that best meet the needs of the larger organization and community.

1. What will other people want to know about the activities and plans of the site team?
2. What will happen if we do not communicate with them on a regular basis?
3. How can we avoid these problems and misconceptions?
4. What strategies will we use? How often will we use these different strategies? How will we know if they are working?

Larry J. Reynolds. *Successful Site-Based Management: A Practical Guide*, rev. ed. Copyright © 1997 by Corwin Press, Inc. Reprinted with permission.

Reviewing and Revising Group Norms

The next step is for the site team to review the initial statement of group norms used in Worksheet 28, Defining the Structure and Membership of the Site Team. It was suggested that the initial listing heavily reflect the behaviors that are required to develop relationships based on trust. The group may also wish to refer to other listings of effective group behaviors to derive its own final listing.

The norms established by the site team should be used in the group's self-evaluation of its communication skills and effectiveness in the future. And, as is suggested in the next section, the facilitator for each site-team meeting should have this list in front of him or her to monitor the process of each meeting. It is also suggested that this list be enlarged and posted in a prominent place so that it is visible to the site-team members during their meetings.

The listing of group norms is not a beginning exercise that is filed away and forgotten. It should be a constant reminder that effective groups have to work at it, all the time. Every second meeting or so, the site team should evaluate itself on its ability to put its own theory into practice.

Worksheet 31 provides a guide to a review and revision of group norms.

Structuring the Site Team for Success

WORKSHEET 31
Reviewing and Revising Group Norms

Step 1: Review and clarify initial listing.

Distribute a copy of the initial statement of group norms from Worksheet 28. Have the members generate examples of the behaviors that would be consistent and inconsistent with each of the statements.

Step 2: Add items as appropriate.

Have the members of the group list additional items that may be perceived as helpful to include. Have other members of the group give concrete examples that would be consistent and inconsistent with each item to see if other members understand what the new item means. By using concrete examples, it should be possible to avoid repeating similar items.

Step 3: Revise for final listing.

Make changes as necessary until the group is comfortable with the listing. Include this listing in the minutes of the meeting and distribute a copy to each member. Make an enlarged copy that can be prominently displayed so that all members of the group can see it during each meeting.

Larry J. Reynolds. *Successful Site-Based Management: A Practical Guide*, rev. ed. Copyright © 1997 by Corwin Press, Inc. Reprinted with permission.

Reviewing External Influences on the Team

Although each member of the team should have become familiar with the purposes of site-based management and the responsibilities of the site team during the selection process, it is important for the site team to review these as a new group. It is critical that everyone be able to answer the question, "Why are we here?"

The first task is to review the expectations and parameters of the district in the adoption of site-based management. The information in Worksheet 27 developed for the site team should be reviewed by the site team, and any questions and concerns addressed. If necessary, the principal should request one of the central office resource persons to work with the group.

Understanding the Context of Change

It is also necessary for the site team to understand the context of change in its own setting. The team needs to acquire a similar frame of reference for thinking about the school, its current issues and problems, and the various special programs and projects that are currently under way and be clear about the role of the other advisory and decision-making groups active in the school. It is suggested that the principal take the lead in this discussion, presenting the information from Worksheets 18, 19, and 20 in Chapter 6. By virtue of this activity, the principal can communicate his or her openness and trust in the site team and build his or her own level of credibility and trust with its members.

The site team must recognize that this discussion is for background information only. At this early stage, the members are not in a position to try and solve any problems of the school. Neither their effectiveness as a decision-making group nor their credibility has been established. What they do need to understand, however, is the following:

- The issues and problems of the school will emerge during the strategic planning process.
- The current special projects and programs will compete for the time and energy of the staff.
- The other advisory and decision-making groups of the school will be concerned about their future role in the school and how their influence and power will be affected by the site team.

By understanding these issues and problems, projects and programs, and role of advisory and decision-making groups, the site-team members can better understand why it is so important for them to understand their larger purposes and the

Structuring the Site Team for Success

timeline for their activities and to communicate these to the school community. They are not responsible for solving any *one* problem nor are they responsible for only *one* program or project. They are, however, responsible for strategic planning, developing a shared vision of the future, and identifying school improvement plans for the future. They will, during this process, be dealing with the specific issues and problems, projects and programs, and advisory and decision-making groups in developing an overall strategy of school improvement with the participation and involvement of the entire school. The site-team members will lead the school according to the timeline and process they develop.

This review is also important for the group itself. Different members of the site team will have their own perceptions of the current status of the school. They may perceive particular issues and problems as particularly critical and needing immediate attention. They may be involved in one or more of the special programs and projects of the school and have reservations about others. They may be members of other school advisory or decision-making groups. Therefore, each member may have his or her own priorities and definition of what the real problem is.

It is important that the group members become aware of each others' perceptions of the context of change. By having each member present his or her current perceptions of the school, including both its strengths and weaknesses, it will be possible for individuals to get this out in the open, contributing to the honesty and trust dimensions of the members' interactions in the group. It will also be an opportunity for the group to practice the norms it has stated for the group, for example, the ability to listen to others. This process should be easier for the group knowing that this information is for the group's development of a shared understanding rather than an attempt to either convince others that their perceptions are right or to resolve issues or problems immediately.

Worksheet 32 is presented as a guide to this discussion.

WORKSHEET 32
Current Perceptions of the Context of Change

Directions: Have the members spend 2 to 3 minutes thinking about their perceptions of the strengths of the school and the problems and issues it faces. Then have each person give one strength and one problem or issue. Ask members to offer items not already listed to get as complete a listing as possible. After going around the group, ask the members if there are other items that they would like to add to the list. Limit each member to no more than three items in each category.

When the list is complete, ask each member whether others offered items in either category that were similar to the items he or she offered. Do not seek agreement or try and prioritize either listing.

The person leading this activity should emphasize that this similarity and diversity of perceptions and opinions will also exist in the larger school community. It will be the future task of the site team to work with that reality and diversity.

School Strengths	*School Problems and Issues*
1. _____	1. _____
2. _____	2. _____
3. _____	3. _____

Larry J. Reynolds. *Successful Site-Based Management: A Practical Guide*, rev. ed. Copyright © 1997 by Corwin Press, Inc. Reprinted with permission.

Selecting Members for Leadership Positions

After the norms, communication needs, purposes, expectations, and parameters of the site team have been reviewed, the site team should select the members who will assume the formal positions of the group.

There are three positions that will help ensure that the site team is an effective one: the group chair, the group facilitator, and the recorder. The chair is primarily responsible for keeping the team on task and setting the schedule of activities and outputs that will allow the team to meet its defined purposes and steps in implementing site-based management. The group facilitator is responsible for monitoring the interaction of the members and reviewing the effectiveness of each meeting in terms of the norms of the group and the accomplishment of the tasks. The group recorder is responsible for ensuring that the internal and external communication needs of the group are met.

As mentioned earlier, it is not recommended that the principal becomes the chair of the group. The first reason is symbolic: A different chair will signal a departure from the previous patterns of control and compliance from the district through the principal. Second, the principal needs to be freed from the responsibilities of running the meetings to focus on the leadership and technical assistance needs of the group. As discussed in Chapter 6, the principal may be the only one in the group who is accustomed to looking at the total school program. Furthermore, as decisions about the instructional program are passed from the principal to the site team, the principal may need to provide a large amount of information to the group on everything ranging from timelines for decisions to state requirements.

Reviewing the Yearly Cycle

The final area in the site team's initial activities is to review the yearly cycle of the school. The members of the site team need to plan their own meetings and work so the team is in sync with the activities and timelines of the yearly school calendar. Two major areas need to be identified:

1. The schedule of activities and events that will compete for the time and attention of the school community

2. The timeline for budget, staffing, and program decisions during the year

All schools operate on a yearly cycle beginning in August, when first principals and then teachers begin the new year. Workshops held before school starts, the excitement and energy level of the new year, and the 2- to 3-week "getting settled in" period are all part of the yearly cycle as well.

At different times during the year, the site team's work will compete for the time and attention of the school staff. A quick review of the yearly calendar will guide the site team in scheduling its own work and its requests for parent, staff, and student involvement.

A yearly cycle also exists with regard to budget, staffing, and program decisions. Budget allocations, proposals for funding different categories of expenditures, and approvals follow a yearly schedule. Staffing allocations, announcing available positions, interviewing candidates, and hiring decisions also follow a yearly timeline. Program decisions must be made in a timely fashion to allow for staff development and the purchasing and delivery of materials and supplies. The program improvement plans of the site team will need to be timed according to the yearly cycle of these decisions as well.

Worksheet 33 is provided as a guide in reviewing the yearly cycle of the school and identifying critical points in the school year. Although most of the information can be derived from the yearly calendar typically prepared by the district, each school will have its own variations. The principal can typically provide the decision-related information.

Structuring the Site Team for Success

WORKSHEET 33
Yearly Cycle of Activities, Events, and Decisions

Fill in the important dates the site team must consider in its own scheduling.

	Aug	Sept	Oct	Nov	Dec	Jan	Feb	Mar	Apr	May	Jun
Teacher workshops	—	—	—	—	—	—	—	—	—	—	—
School starts	—	—	—	—	—	—	—	—	—	—	—
Grading periods	—	—	—	—	—	—	—	—	—	—	—
Parent conferences	—	—	—	—	—	—	—	—	—	—	—
End of year	—	—	—	—	—	—	—	—	—	—	—
Special events	—	—	—	—	—	—	—	—	—	—	—
Vacations	—	—	—	—	—	—	—	—	—	—	—
Other	—	—	—	—	—	—	—	—	—	—	—
	—	—	—	—	—	—	—	—	—	—	—
Budget process	—	—	—	—	—	—	—	—	—	—	—
Staffing decisions	—	—	—	—	—	—	—	—	—	—	—
Program decisions	—	—	—	—	—	—	—	—	—	—	—

Larry J. Reynolds. *Successful Site-Based Management: A Practical Guide*, rev. ed. Copyright © 1997 by Corwin Press, Inc. Reprinted with permission.

Summary

Considerable attention has been given to discussing the initial activities of the site team. It is important to stress that unless this investment is made for the future, the site team will rush into "doing something" and leave a number of important issues unresolved. Unless the site team completes these steps, it will find that both its efficiency and effectiveness will soon suffer.

The following chapter will focus on the new skills the site team will need to develop prior to beginning its strategic planning activities.

9

Learning New Skills

Training in new skills is an important "forming" activity for the site team. The training will increase the amount of interaction time of the new group members and increase their base of common experiences. In addition, the training is a key part of the norm-setting process for the group, helping to define how the group is going to work together in the future.

As a basic service, the central office and the site team's own facilitator can provide important resources to the team. Because all new teams in the district will require training in new skills, the district can use its personnel to plan and provide a training program for the facilitators for site teams across the district. Through this service, the central office can demonstrate its commitment to site-based management and build its credibility and trust with the site teams. It is suggested that the site teams receive training, under the leadership of the site team's own facilitator, in the following areas that are essential to the effective interaction among members during their meetings: listening skills, discussion skills, conflict resolution skills, and feedback skills.

In this chapter, the discussion will focus on three additional skills that are critical for the effectiveness and success of the site team in school improvement efforts:

- Leadership skills
- Strategic planning skills
- Problem-solving and decision-making skills

Leadership Skills

In Chapter 2, it was stated that site-based management needs to emphasize a leadership perspective as opposed to a management perspective. Furthermore, the leadership perspective is required of central office personnel, the building principal, and the school site team. If significant improvements are to be made in the instructional program of the school to increase the success of students, then the efforts of all three levels need to be consistent and coordinated. The site team must understand that the leadership perspectives and behaviors that are required of central office personnel and the principal are also required of the site team.

The differences between management and leadership, as identified by Kotter (1990), should be clearly understood by the site team. These differences were summarized in Table 2.1 on page 10.

For the site team to be perceived by others as having a legitimate leadership role in the school, the individual members of the site team and the site team as a group will have to demonstrate the same four leadership characteristics required of others in the district assuming leadership roles. These characteristics and their definitions were discussed in Table 2.2 on page 11. An important activity for the site team is to generate a listing of the specific behaviors and styles of interaction with others that will promote each of the required leadership characteristics of the team. To prepare for this activity, site-team members may want to review the discussion in Chapter 7 on the specific behaviors of the principal that can build credibility, trust, vision, and inspiration. This activity also provides an opportunity for the principal to lead a discussion on the overall leadership requirements of site-based management and how the leadership behaviors of the principal and site team can reinforce each other.

Worksheet 34 is provided as a guide in defining leadership behaviors for the site team. The site team may want to periodically review a summary of Worksheet 34 to see if the leadership behaviors it defined during its forming activities are actually being implemented by team members.

Learning New Skills

WORKSHEET 34
Developing Site-Team Leadership

Generate as many ideas as you can for how the site team
can meet each of the requirements of leadership.

Leadership Characteristics	Specific Site-Team Behaviors
Vision	_____
	_____
	_____
	_____
Trust	_____
	_____
	_____
	_____
Credibility	_____
	_____
	_____
	_____
Inspiration	_____
	_____
	_____
	_____

Larry J. Reynolds. *Successful Site-Based Management: A Practical Guide*, rev. ed. Copyright © 1997 by Corwin Press, Inc. Reprinted with permission.

Strategic Planning Skills

It is of utmost importance that the site team learn strategic planning skills. It must not only be aware of and responsive to the strategic planning done at the district level, but it must demonstrate its own understanding and skill at the building level. The central office is frequently reluctant to delegate decisions to principals and to building groups because individuals at that level do not understand the big picture. An important part of our strategy has been to get the central office to define and communicate the big picture. The second part of this strategy is for the site team to be responsive to the big picture.

As discussed in Chapter 2, strategic planning is a process for looking at where you are, where you want to go, and what it will take to get there. It allows a focus on the total school program, provides a sense of control over the future, and allows the organization to be responsive to a constantly changing environment of needs and demands.

There are six steps in strategic planning.

1. Identify the external forces, current and future, acting on the district and its schools.

2. Define the nature of the client population and its current and future needs.

3. Clarify the values and beliefs of participants about education.

4. Create a shared vision of the future.

5. Assess the strengths and weaknesses of the program.

6. Set priorities and plan program improvements.

The site team must be knowledgeable about both the content of the strategic planning already accomplished at the district level and the process of strategic planning for its own future activities. Worksheet 35 is presented as a guide for the review of the first part of the strategic planning model. The major task for the site team is to determine how the individual school "fits" the overall district description and vision. Specifically, there are four questions to be asked.

1. Which of the external forces (or trends) are most pertinent to our school and will be most critical in the future?

2. Which of the student needs are most pertinent to our school and students?

3. Which educational beliefs and values are most critical for us to consider?

4. Which vision components are most likely to need special attention in our school?

WORKSHEET 35
Review of the Districtwide Strategic Plan

For each of the following components of the districtwide strategic plan, determine those parts that are most important to your school. Note any additions to each that will be important considerations in the strategic planning at the school level.

Component of Districtwide Strategic Plan	*Areas of Special Importance to Our School*
External forces	_____ _____ _____
Student needs	_____ _____ _____
Beliefs and values	_____ _____ _____
Vision	_____
Organizational climate Program organization Classroom interactions	_____ _____

Larry J. Reynolds. *Successful Site-Based Management: A Practical Guide*, rev. ed. Copyright © 1997 by Corwin Press, Inc. Reprinted with permission.

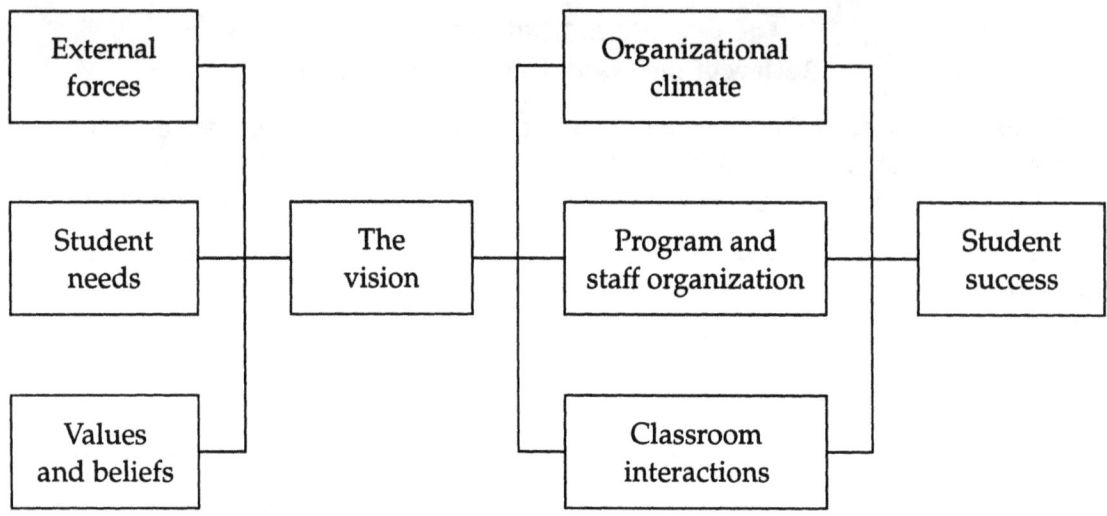

Figure 9.1. School-Level Strategic Planning Model

By addressing these four questions, the site team will be better able to lead the school community in strategic planning and anticipate some of the issues that may arise during the process. Worksheet 35 is provided as a tool for the site team to use in reviewing the districtwide strategic planning. The strategic planning model that will be used at the school level is provided in Figure 9.1 for reference.

Problem-Solving and Decision-Making Skills

The problem solving and decision making of the site team will come into play after the shared vision of the educational program and services of the school has been generated by the school community. In the context of the vision, problems will be defined as follows:

$$\begin{array}{r} \text{The vision (desired level)} \\ - \text{ The present (current level)} \\ \hline \text{The problem (the difference)} \end{array}$$

The problem may not necessarily be negative. If continuous improvement is the goal of the school, then the problem may be how to increase the effectiveness of the school program beyond levels that are already perceived as satisfactory, or even excellent. Or the problem may be to attain a new set of goals for the school. The problem can occur at any current level of performance by a student, a group of students, or the school as a whole as long as the desired level is an improvement.

The efficiency and effectiveness of the site team in developing school improvement plans will be dependent on its ability to follow a predetermined sequence of steps in problem solving and decision making. Groups are frequently criticized because "all they do is talk about problems; they never do anything about them" or the decision was predetermined and the discussion was for show. It is critical for the site-team members to have a sense of accomplishment in their activities that can be derived by completing the steps. The sequence of steps we suggested below is designed to be employed whenever the group is trying to solve problems and to decide on school improvement strategies:

1. Defining the problem
2. Identifying the causes of the problem
3. Generating alternative solutions
4. Evaluating and selecting alternatives
5. Implementing solutions

Defining the Problem

When we talk about problems, frequently our personal point of view or concerns cause us to be less than objective and specific about their nature. In education, we say "The students are ___." Or "The teachers aren't ___." Or "If only the administration would ___." Or "Why can't parents ___." Our frustration level with each others' actions does not help us to be very precise, or sometimes very accurate, in how we perceive different problems. And, if we are having trouble being listened to, our concerns intensify and our objectivity declines even further.

An important first step for the site team is to carefully define the problem that requires its attention. Worksheet 36 suggests a series of questions to ask when examining an initial statement of a problem. Focusing on what the problem is and is not will bring increased specificity to a restatement of the problem. And, by examining the differences between what is and what is not the problem, the site team may gain some important insights into the potential causes of the problem.

WORKSHEET 36
Defining the Problem

Initial problem statement: _____
_____
_____

	Is	Is Not	Differences
Who?	_____	_____	_____
What?	_____	_____	_____
When?	_____	_____	_____
Where?	_____	_____	_____
How?	_____	_____	_____
Why?	_____	_____	_____
How much?	_____	_____	_____

Redefined problem statement: _____
_____
_____

Larry J. Reynolds. *Successful Site-Based Management: A Practical Guide*, rev. ed. Copyright © 1997 by Corwin Press, Inc. Reprinted with permission.

Identifying the Causes of Problems

One of the "problems" of problems is that they usually involve people. We may be reluctant to admit that a problem exists or defensive about why we have a problem or why we are the source of someone else's problem. It is easy to make excuses, deny that the problem really exists, or blame others. An example follows.

Problem Example: John can't read.

> John's reading achievement is well below grade level. He is not interested in reading and fails to pay attention during reading class. He frequently misbehaves at this time, resulting in the teacher sending him to the office. John does not qualify for special programs, tutors, or other assistance. The problem is viewed in the following ways by different people.
>
> The teacher feels John has a poor attitude. His parents don't really care; they never return the teacher's phone calls or respond to notes asking them to help John with his extra reading at home. The teacher does not have time to work with John individually. Also, the teacher does not have the knowledge and skills to really understand John's reading problem or the materials that might be of assistance. John has been sent to the office numerous times, but the principal always sends him back and his behavior hasn't changed.
>
> The principal is tired of seeing John in the office. He feels the teacher should be more effective working with students like John and that John can't learn when he is out of class. John's parents both work and it is difficult to get them to respond to the principal's calls during the day.
>
> John's parents can't understand why John is having a problem this year. He has not had any problems in reading in the past. They do know, however, that John does not like his teacher. They would be glad to help John at home if they just knew what to do.
>
> John doesn't understand what the big deal is.

As is frequently the case, the nature of the problem depends on who you ask. And the solutions offered by different persons are frequently prefaced by the words *if only*. "If only the student would ___." "If only the parents would ___."

The difficulties with this approach are obvious. Instead, it is necessary to move beyond talking about people and begin describing the attitudes and behaviors of people that need to be changed. Second, it is necessary for people to see that there is frequently more than one cause for a problem's existence and that it may take more than one strategy to really solve the problem.

Two approaches to identify the causes of problems are suggested. The first of these approaches uses a "fishbone" diagram to locate the sources of problems as expressed through the attitudes and behaviors of individuals. The second fishbone diagram locates the causes of problems in different categories of influences such as time and scheduling, interest and motivation, knowledge and skills, and materials and equipment. Although either approach may be used in problem solving, one or the other may be more helpful in certain instances. Furthermore, the group may find that different categories might need to be explored. The important thing is to begin to list all of the potential causes of a problem so that you can move to the next step of identifying solutions.

These two diagrams are presented in Worksheet 37. The next step is to combine the information from the two diagrams in Worksheet 38. This will summarize the information, linking people and behaviors, allowing potential solutions to be identified for the problem.

Learning New Skills 137

WORKSHEET 37
Identifying the Causes of Problems

Generate as many potential causes as you can for each problem.

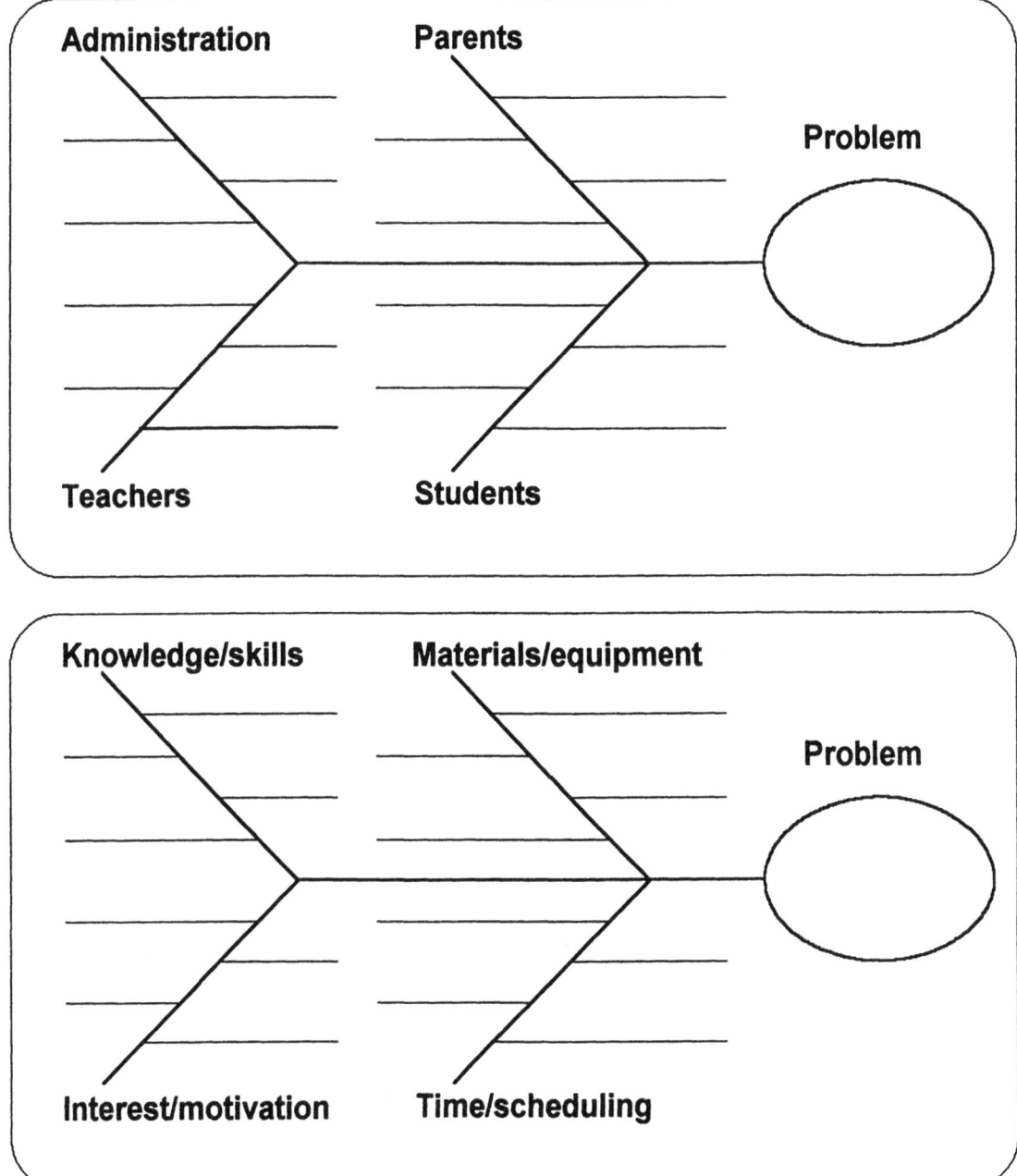

Place a star (*) by the five most powerful causes.

Larry J. Reynolds. *Successful Site-Based Management: A Practical Guide*, rev. ed. Copyright © 1997 by Corwin Press, Inc. Reprinted with permission.

WORKSHEET 38
Summarizing the Causes of Problems

Problem statement:

_____

_____

	Knowledge and Skills	Materials and Equipment	Interest and Motivation	Time and Scheduling
Students	_____	_____	_____	_____
	_____	_____	_____	_____
Parents	_____	_____	_____	_____
	_____	_____	_____	_____
Teachers	_____	_____	_____	_____
	_____	_____	_____	_____
Administrators	_____	_____	_____	_____
	_____	_____	_____	_____
Other	_____	_____	_____	_____
	_____	_____	_____	_____

Larry J. Reynolds. *Successful Site-Based Management: A Practical Guide*, rev. ed. Copyright © 1997 by Corwin Press, Inc. Reprinted with permission.

Brainstorming Possible Solutions

Once the causes of the problem have been identified, it is possible to begin to brainstorm solutions. It is important to locate the causes over which the members of the school community have some degree of influence or control. It would be nice, perhaps, if both of John's parents did not have to work. They could then spend more time with John helping him with his reading. But the school has little control over whether John's parents work. The time might be better spent finding ways to get John interested in reading.

Worksheet 39 provides a guide for generating potential solutions to a problem by identifying the causes of the problem.

WORKSHEET 39
Brainstorming Possible Solutions

Problem statement: _____

_____

Causes of Problem	Potential Solutions
1.	
2.	
3.	
4.	
5.	

Larry J. Reynolds. *Successful Site-Based Management: A Practical Guide*, rev. ed. Copyright © 1997 by Corwin Press, Inc. Reprinted with permission.

Learning New Skills

Evaluating and Selecting Alternatives

It is now possible to evaluate the possible solutions to the problem in terms of their advantages and disadvantages. The site team will want to generate a listing of these as well as create a set of criteria for all potential solutions. The following changes are suggested in Worksheet 40.

- Cost: What investment is required for teacher training, supervision, and coordination; materials and equipment; or extra staff?
- Time: What will be the time demands on different individuals, and how long will it take to change schedules and prepare and receive new equipment and materials?
- Complexity: How difficult will it be to coordinate all the different activities and people involved, how great a change in behavior will it require, and what new knowledge and skills will have to be learned?
- Effect: How significant an effect will this solution have on the problem?
- Acceptance: How acceptable will this solution be to parents, teachers, students, and administrators?
- Risk: What can go wrong, and what will the consequences be if this strategy does not work?

Worksheet 40 also provides a scoring system to rank the alternatives in terms of these criteria.

Implementing Solutions

The last step is to determine the strategy for implementing the selected solutions. It will be important to identify "who will do what and by when" and to determine how the site team will monitor the progress of the solutions that it has decided on. By using a simple worksheet, it will be easier to receive information on progress and take corrective steps if the strategy is not being implemented as intended.

Worksheet 41 provides a guide to defining these components of the implementation strategy.

WORKSHEET 40
Evaluating and Selecting Alternatives

Problem statement: _____

Possible solutions to solve problem	Advantages	Disadvantages
1. _____	_____	_____
2. _____	_____	_____
3. _____	_____	_____
4. _____	_____	_____
5. _____	_____	_____

Evaluation criteria: Circle one. Top row most desirable.

Solution	Cost	Time	Complexity	Effect	Acceptance	Risk	Scores	Total and Rank
1.	Low	Short	Low	High	High	Low	3s __	Total
	Medium	Medium	Medium	Medium	Medium	Medium	2s __	_____
	High	Long	High	Low	Low	High	1s __	Rank
2.	Low	Short	Low	High	High	Low	3s __	Total
	Medium	Medium	Medium	Medium	Medium	Medium	2s __	_____
	High	Long	High	Low	Low	High	1s __	Rank
3.	Low	Short	Low	High	High	Low	3s __	Total
	Medium	Medium	Medium	Medium	Medium	Medium	2s __	_____
	High	Long	High	Low	Low	High	1s __	Rank
4.	Low	Short	Low	High	High	Low	3s __	Total
	Medium	Medium	Medium	Medium	Medium	Medium	2s __	_____
	High	Long	High	Low	Low	High	1s __	Rank
5.	Low	Short	Low	High	High	Low	3s __	Total
	Medium	Medium	Medium	Medium	Medium	Medium	2s __	_____
	High	Long	High	Low	Low	High	1s __	Rank

Larry J. Reynolds. *Successful Site-Based Management: A Practical Guide*, rev. ed. Copyright © 1997 by Corwin Press, Inc. Reprinted with permission.

Learning New Skills

WORKSHEET 41
Implementing Solutions

Problem statement: _____

_____

Solution: _____

Activities	Person Responsible	Time of Completion
1. _____	_____	_____
2. _____	_____	_____
3. _____	_____	_____
4. _____	_____	_____
5. _____	_____	_____

Larry J. Reynolds. *Successful Site-Based Management: A Practical Guide*, rev. ed. Copyright © 1997 by Corwin Press, Inc. Reprinted with permission.

Summary

The five steps suggested for problem solving and decision making, and the worksheets provided, may appear to involve a lengthy and detailed process. The worksheets are intended as an initial guide to the team, one that can certainly be condensed as members of the team increase their efficiency in this area. Going through all the steps initially, however, does provide some distinct advantages to the team in the long run.

1. The worksheets will provide a structure to group discussions, preventing the discussions from going in circles.

2. Using the worksheets will force the group to consider multiple ideas about causes and solutions to problems, decreasing the chance of a few people dominating the group with their perceptions and ideas.

3. The worksheets will provide the group with a sense of movement and accomplishment. The discussion of some issues and problems will certainly require more than one meeting, and it will be important for the group to be able to define for itself, and others, the progress that has been made.

4. The worksheets provide a division of labor for subgroups or subcommittees that may be formed by the site team. By using the worksheets, it is possible to define clearly the task of the subgroup and the information required by the site team.

5. Finally, the worksheets and process document the work of the site team and the rationale it has used in decision making.

In the next chapter, the focus is on the strategic planning process for the school and the leadership role and activities of the site team.

10

Working With the School Community

Thus far, the discussion has covered the relationship of the site team with the central office and the principal and the formation and training of the site team. The focus of this chapter shifts to the actual work of the site team and its relationship with the school community of staff, parents, and students.

The purpose of the site team has been defined earlier in terms of its role in both the strategic planning and decision-making structure of the school district. Its purpose is to develop a shared vision of the educational program and services of the individual school, identify priorities for school improvement, and evaluate the effectiveness of school improvement strategies in terms of the shared vision. The effectiveness of the site team in pursuing these responsibilities depends in great part on its relationship with the larger school community. How others perceive the site team is critical.

The image of the site team will be established by the attitude it communicates about its role in the school and its relationships with others. The norms and values of the group will become apparent almost immediately. The success of the site team can be enhanced to the degree that the following "messages" are sent to the school community from the beginning:

1. The site team is concerned about the future of the school and its programs and services. Its purpose is not to criticize or defend either the past successes or failures of the school program, groups, or individuals.

2. The site team believes in the full participation of others based on trust, respect, and a commitment to common goals.

3. The site team is committed to collaboration with others in the development of a shared vision and school improvement plans.

4. The site team believes in a customer focus with a goal of continuous improvement in the programs and services for students and parents.

These attitudes and commitments of the site team, as individuals and as a group, can be demonstrated in its first major activity with the school community—building a shared vision of the future.

The Importance of a Shared Vision of the Future

The shared vision of the school is the key document, reference point, guide to action, and shared commitment of the site team. The purpose of the shared vision is to set the overall direction for the activities and decisions of the site team. It provides the common language to be used in discussions about the educational programs and services of the school. It is, in short, both an ideal picture of the future and a working document for the present.

It is important to repeat what the vision is and is not. The vision is not the same as a mission statement, that is, a one-sentence statement of what the school is trying to accomplish. The vision is a descriptive document that states, in terms of activities, interactions, and values, what the school experience should be for students, parents, and staff. For our purposes, it is divided into three parts: the organizational climate of the school, the organization of the educational program, and the nature of classroom interactions.

As an example of the differences between a mission statement and a vision, the site team could develop its own mission statement. It might be stated as follows:

> The mission of the site team is to build the confidence and ability of the school to make continuous improvements in its educational programs and services and in the success of its students.

The mission statement, however, does not state what it is like to be a member of the site team. It does not describe how the site team is organized, its norms and values, how site-team members will interact, what strategies will be used for decision making, and so on. What has been presented in Chapter 9 in the discussion of the site team's structure and training is, in essence, a vision of effective site teams.

Because of the importance of the shared vision of the school, it is the first major activity of the site team. It requires the broad participation of members of the school community and is a major event. It can be an exciting, challenging opportunity to bring the school community together in a shared activity and create a positive and confident commitment to the future success of the school and its students.

Accomplishing the Task

The task of the site team is to lead the school community through a strategic planning process that produces a shared vision of the future excellence of the individual school. It is achieved through the same process that was completed at the district level (see Chapter 4). The first step of the process for the school community is the same activity that was recommended for the site team in Chapter 9 (see Worksheet 35), that is, a review of the districtwide vision and its three influencing factors (external forces, the needs of students, and values and beliefs about education). This review was designed to familiarize the site team with the strategic planning model and the earlier work at the district level. The additional task now is to add the building's shared vision.

It is important to stress that the school community is not expected to approve, disapprove, or modify the districtwide vision. It is a given. The expectations for the school community are to refine and extend the work at the district level so that it is appropriate for the more specific circumstances and needs of the individual school.

The school community should be involved in all six steps of the strategic planning process.

1. Identifying the external forces, current and future, acting on the school.
2. Defining the nature of the client population and its current and future needs.
3. Clarifying the values and beliefs of participants about education.
4. Creating a shared vision of the future.
5. Assessing the strengths and weaknesses of the program.
6. Setting priorities and planning program improvements.

Strategic planning in a large group is a time-consuming process. It is recommended that Steps 1 through 4 be completed as Phase 1, that Step 5 and the first part of Step 6 be completed as Phase 2, and that the last part of Step 6 be completed as Phase 3.

It is further recommended that the site team select a large group for participation in Phase 1 and Phase 2. Smaller, specially formed groups can best work on special program improvement plans in Phase 3, although these groups should provide for representatives from and continued involvement of the total school community.

Participation

The site team should schedule either a full day (or 2 half days) for Phase 1 and a full day for Phase 2. The scheduling of Phase 3 will depend on the specific task and group involved. The strategic planning workshop will most likely require released time for staff or the use of the planning days of the school. The involvement of parents is made more difficult because of work schedules. (A letter or a phone call by the principal to employers stating the purpose of the workshop and the school's interest in parent and community involvement may be one way to facilitate obtaining the time to participate in this important event.)

The following should be considered in selecting participants. First, parents and the general community must be involved in sufficient numbers to add credibility to the process and to provide valid input from their perspectives. They will provide diversity, and that is their value. The school, principals, and staff deal with these diverse opinions every day, frequently in a problem-centered format. This input needs to be received in a collaborative and planning setting as well. Of particular value will be those community members who interact with students in nonschool settings. They will know things about the students and the program that may be different, surprising, and insightful.

Second, all school staff should be included, professional and nonprofessional. The goal is to build a commitment to the shared vision, and everyone's opinion and contribution should be valued. Furthermore, the school staff will be, ultimately, the major actors in the implementation of school improvement plans.

Third, nonprofessional staff will have a powerful contribution to make to this process. Their interactions with students are different from those of the professional staff. Furthermore, these are the people who interact with the community both in and out of school. Their perceptions will be especially insightful in the area of school climate.

Fourth, students should be included at the secondary level. They are the only ones who experience the total school program on a day-by-day basis. The students selected for participation should be as diverse as the student body itself; this is not the time or place to recognize only the school's merit scholars or student government leaders.

Phase 1: Creating the Shared Vision

The setting should be as comfortable as possible with tables and chairs arranged for small groups of approximately 8 to 10 people. The day's schedule should provide for an informal period for interaction with refreshments for participants before the formal workshop begins. A short break in the middle of the morning and afternoon should be scheduled as well as a reasonable lunch break if appropriate. Have a nonworking lunch together if at all possible at the workshop site.

The membership of each small group should be planned in advance by the site team and indicated by name cards at each table. The goal is to have an equal number of representatives of each group of participants at each table. This is not the time for cliques to sit together or for parents or students to be isolated at one or more tables. Faculty should not be arranged by department or grade level. The participants who have formal and informal leadership status should be mixed among groups. If possible, a member of the site team should be the facilitator at each table. Additional facilitators, if needed, should be indicated by the site team.

The first activity should be to clarify the overall role and function of the site team and clearly define the purpose of the day's workshop. The facilitators should be briefed in advance on how to lead the group's discussions to increase their effectiveness, and these ground rules should be stated to the large group before the small groups begin their work. The expected product of the workshop should be specified as well as how it will be used in the future. In other words, the strategic planning process needs to be reviewed before work is begun.

It is important to note that the concept of strategic planning may appear to some participants as a very difficult, esoteric task that has little relevance to the present and to immediate concerns. It is important to stress that the components of the strategic planning model we suggest are the very things that people talk about when they talk about the schools. Teachers, students, parents, and other members of the community talk about changes in the neighborhood, about the need for a new building or additional classrooms, about bond issues and tax levies, about what is important to teach, about budget issues, and so on. These are very real interests and concerns of the members of the school community that influence their expectations for the educational program and services of the school and their levels of satisfaction with the school.

It will be critical for the large group to understand that the product of the workshop will become a working document for the school. This is not to be a meaningless activity that results in a thick document that is retired to a shelf or a filing cabinet. If this has been the experience of the participants for similar activities in the past, the site team must establish why this work is different. The quality of the work during the workshop will be influenced by the extent to which the participants truly believe this. Explaining the future use of the shared vision in identifying school improvement needs will help. Instructions for Activity 1 are provided below.

Activity 1: Review of the Districtwide Strategic Plan

The purpose of this activity is to give the large-group members an opportunity to study the districtwide plan, determine its particular relevance to their own school, and begin to think in terms of the vision categories. Each group should have a copy of the districtwide strategic planning output and should answer the following four questions:

1. Which of the external forces (or trends) are most pertinent to our school and will be most critical in the future?
2. Which of the student needs are most pertinent to our school and students?
3. Which educational beliefs and values are most critical for us to consider?
4. Which vision components are most likely to need special attention in our school?

Using Worksheet 42, each small group should do the following:

1. Each member should spend about 10 minutes thinking about the questions and each category of response.
2. The facilitator should then go around the group, taking each question in turn, and ask each member to give one item that he or she considers important. Each response should be recorded on large newsprint. The group should be allowed 20 to 30 minutes for this activity.
3. After the group has generated responses to each of the questions, it can select the two or three items it would like to report out to the total group. Continue around the group as many times as possible, asking for additions and combining items when possible. These should be circled on the newsprint and given to the facilitator of the workshop at the end of the session. Allow 2 to 3 minutes for each group to report out.
4. The responses of each small group should be recorded on large newsprint to be later summarized by the site team.

5. The facilitator of the workshop should reemphasize the purposes of this activity and that it serves as a "warm-up" for the work of the next activity—generating a shared vision of the future excellence of the school.

If the district has not developed a strategic plan or has not made this information available to the individual school, the workshop should do its own strategic planning anyway. The workshop should then focus on the sequence of events described for the districtwide group in Chapter 4.

WORKSHEET 42
Review of the Districtwide Strategic Plan (by the School Community)

For each of the following components of the districtwide strategic plan, determine those parts that are most important to your school. Note any additions to each that will be important considerations in the strategic planning at the school level.

Component of Districtwide Strategic Plan	Areas of Special Importance to Our School
External forces	_____ _____ _____
Student needs	_____ _____ _____
Beliefs and values	_____ _____ _____
Vision categories	_____
Organizational climate	_____
Program plan	_____
Classroom interactions	_____

Larry J. Reynolds. *Successful Site-Based Management: A Practical Guide,* rev. ed. Copyright © 1997 by Corwin Press, Inc. Reprinted with permission.

Activity 2: Generating the Shared Vision

Using Worksheet 43 as a guide, the group should do the following:

1. Allow individuals to spend from 10 to 15 minutes thinking about each of the vision categories and their ideas about what it would be like for students, parents, and staff in the ideal school.

2. The facilitator should then go around the group, taking each area of the vision in turn, and ask each member to give one item that he or she considers important. Continue around the group as many times as possible, asking for additions and combining items when possible. Each item should be recorded on large newsprint. The group should allow 20 to 30 minutes for this activity.

3. After the group has generated responses to each of the questions, it can select the two or three items in each category it would like to report out. One way to determine the selected items is for each member to have two or three votes for his or her choices and to select those items with the highest total. These should be circled on the groups newsprint. Allow the groups 20 to 30 minutes for this activity.

4. Have each group report out two or three items from any category or combination of categories it chooses. It is important for the total group to hear the responses of the other groups. Participants will recognize similarities in the responses of other groups, and this will help build the consensus needed for the final document. Allow 5 minutes for each group.

5. The responses of each small group should be recorded on large newsprint to be finalized in the next activity.

6. The facilitator should reemphasize the purposes of this activity and review the next steps in the production of the "final" shared vision.

The completion of this activity ends the large group's involvement in Phase 1.

Activity 3: Finalizing the Shared Vision

The next step in the generation of the shared vision is to take the input of the large group and to produce and edit a final listing for each category of the vision. This should be done by a subgroup composed of one member from each of the small groups. It can be the facilitator of the group (which would include the site-team members) or it can be a person chosen by each small group. The subgroup will need about a half day to complete the shared vision.

WORKSHEET 43
The Shared Vision (by the School Community)

In the space below, indicate your ideas of the ideal school and program for each of the three major categories. Use short statements that describe what it is like for parents, students, and staff.

Organizational climate: What are the behaviors, activities, and interactions that make up the daily life of the school. What defines the "personality" of the school as a place to learn, work, and visit.

Program plan: How students and staff are arranged for instruction. How you use electives, requirements, schedules, magnets, classes, counseling, advisers, teaming, curriculum integration, and support staff to structure the program. The outcome goals desired such as critical thinking, problem solving, creativity, and basic knowledge and skills.

Classroom interactions: How you view students and learning in terms of both process and content. Includes considerations of student learning styles, self-concept, success, interactions, and activities in instruction as well as outcome goals of critical thinking, problem solving, creativity, and basic knowledge and skills.

Larry J. Reynolds. *Successful Site-Based Management: A Practical Guide*, rev. ed. Copyright © 1997 by Corwin Press, Inc. Reprinted with permission.

Working With the School Community

The current task is to study the large number of items offered by each group in the workshop. The subcommittee should begin by listing those items presented verbally at the workshop by each group, and then add any remaining items selected by the small groups that were not offered in the larger session. The listing may be either fairly compact because of similarities among the small groups, or it may be rather long because of the differences among the small groups. Regardless, the task is now to first produce a complete listing.

The second step is to narrow the listing down to a manageable number for each category of the vision. The subgroup will have to determine what level of detail is required to accurately communicate the major themes of the larger group. It is important to remember that the shared vision is a working document and a guide to action. It is not necessary for it to be the all-time, most complete, and ultimate statement in the world about quality education. The shared vision is a means to attain other goals, and it is important that it be completed in a timely fashion and communicated in its completed form back to the workshop group.

Using a multiple-voting technique, each member of the subcommittee should vote for his or her first, second, and third choices for the most important items in each category. This will produce a scoring for each item, as shown below, and indicate the combined priorities of the group.

Vision category: _____

Item Number	Votes Per Choice	Total Points
1.	1 × ___	
	2 × ___	
	3 × ___	

A final listing of reasonable length can now be completed for each category.

In voting for the final listing of items, it will be important to remember that the shared vision of the school must meet the parameters established by the strategic planning at the district level.

1. Is the vision responsive to external forces?
2. Does the vision meet the needs of students?
3. Is the vision consistent with the values and beliefs about education?
4. Is the vision consistent with the districtwide vision?

The final step for the site team is to produce a document that summarizes the work of the participants in the large-group workshop and the subsequent work of the subgroup. The document is one of the outputs for which the site team is held responsible by the central office. The format of Worksheets 42 and 43 can be used as a guide in producing a summary report to the central office, the workshop participants, and the larger school community.

Phase 2: The Current Program and Priorities for the Future

Phase 2 is designed to "put the vision to work" at the building level. The next two steps in the strategic planning process are to assess the strengths and weaknesses of the current program and to identify priorities for improvement. The same large group of Phase 1 is reconvened for another full-day workshop (or 2 half days). Bringing the large group together again serves four purposes:

1. It provides a sense of accomplishment for members of the school community by seeing that their previous work has resulted in a completed vision of the future and it is being used to identify school improvement needs.

2. It increases the credibility of the site team's leadership role and its commitment to participation and collaboration in decision making.

3. It reinforces using the vision as a guide to action and the common language of the school when talking about the school improvement.

4. It communicates trust and confidence in the larger school community to work cooperatively toward common goals.

Using the same small groups and format, the workshop facilitator should explain that the group's activities will be to continue the strategic planning process. The next areas to be completed are the following:

1. Given the shared vision, the group will first identify those areas of the school program that are strengths of the school and come closest to meeting the vision.

2. Given the vision, the group will then identify those areas of the school program that need further development in the future to attain the vision.

3. Given the initial listing of areas of potential development in the future, the group will select those that are current priorities.

4. Given the priorities for future development, the group will begin to generate ideas for school improvement priorities.

Activity 1: Identifying Current Program Strengths

Each participant should have a copy of the finalized, shared vision in a format similar to that of Worksheet 43 with the items in each category numbered. The workshop facilitator should lead the groups as follows:

1. Allow individuals to spend about 5 minutes reviewing the vision and comparing it to their perceptions of the current school program.

2. The facilitator of each small group should go around the group asking each member to identify one vision item or statement that he or she thinks is a strength of the current school program. Continue around the table until each member has been able to identify two or three different areas of current strength.

3. After the group has identified the areas that individual members perceive as program strengths, have the group identify its top three program strengths. Circle the group's choices on a copy of the vision provided for the use of the group as a whole.

4. Ask the group to think about its top three choices and what has occurred in the school to allow those areas to be real strengths of the current program.

5. Have each group report out two or three items from any category or combination of categories it chooses. Ask each group to share its ideas about why that area is a school strength; that is, what is happening in the school to make it possible to attain that part of the vision?

6. It is important for the total group to hear the responses of other groups. The responses of each group should be recorded on newsprint and displayed before the group. Allow 5 to 10 minutes for each group, depending on the size of the large group.

Activity 2: Identifying Areas for Future Development

This area is purposefully not called "current program weaknesses." It will be important for the principal of the school, the site team, and the workshop facilitator all to stress that one of the major goals of site-based management is continuous improvement. The areas needing development may be new areas of the vision because of different demands on the school or because of an interest in responding to new developments in teaching strategies or instructional technology. It is important for the workshop facilitator to remind people that the vision and the future is the focus, not the performance of individuals or groups in the past.

It would be helpful for the facilitator to have a large poster-size copy of the vision, or a high-quality overhead transparency, that can be easily viewed by the large group and used for the summary discussions in this activity.

The workshop facilitator should lead the group as follows:

1. Allow individuals about 5 minutes to review the vision, thinking about those areas that need further development in the future.

2. The facilitator should then go around the group asking each member to identify one area that he or she sees as needing further development. Continue around the group until each person has had a chance to mention at least two different areas. The facilitator should allow 30 minutes for this activity.

3. After the group members have generated their individual responses, have the group select three items or statements of the vision, from any category or combination of categories, that it feels are priorities for future development.

4. Have each group report the three items it has selected. It is important for the total group to hear the responses of the other groups. This will acquaint participants with a wider range of perceptions than just those from their group. Areas that are repeated will give the larger group a sense of the potential consensus of the group for selecting priorities in the next step. Allow 5 minutes for each group.

5. The responses of each small group should be recorded on a large copy of the vision sheet visible to the entire group. At this point, it is only necessary to record how many times each item in the vision is mentioned.

6. The facilitator should reinforce the idea that these are all areas of potential development in the future. However, the effectiveness of school improvement efforts can be increased by identifying which are areas with the greatest need for attention, which is the purpose of the next activity.

Activity 3: Selecting Current Priorities

The task now is to consider the previous discussions and listing of program development needs and to select those needing the most attention. The workshop facilitator should lead the groups to do the following:

1. Allow each small group to spend 15 to 20 minutes identifying the top three areas in each vision category it considers to be current priorities. They can be the same as those the group identified as its own priorities, or they may have changed now that the group has heard the ideas and perceptions of other groups.

2. The workshop facilitator should then ask each group to give its top three priorities for each category of the vision. The responses of each group should be recorded on another large copy of the school vision so that everyone can see the results of the voting. The number of votes and the point values for each area should be recorded. After all the groups have indicated their choices, then the totals for each area can be calculated.

The group has now identified its priorities for future development. It is suggested that this conclude the half-day workshop. It should be clear to everyone that the next step is to reconvene the same group to get ideas on how the school can improve in these areas.

Activity 4: Generating Ideas for School Improvement Priorities

It will be important for the workshop facilitator to remind everyone in the large group that if school improvement is the shared goal, then everyone is also responsible for helping it to occur. Site-based management is based on shared responsibility. In short, the group also gets to work on how to accomplish its priorities for school improvement.

It is important to stress that the goal of this session is to provide input to the site team in developing program improvement plans for the future. The group is not expected to finalize strategies in this setting, but the site team will be involving the larger school community in refining these plans in the future. The assembled group can help the site team begin its work today.

The large-group facilitator should lead the large group through the following:

1. Allow each group to spend 10 minutes identifying one priority to work on the rest of the session. Have the groups refer to Worksheet 44 to see the kind of work they will be doing. Let them know that each small group will tell the larger group the priority they have selected and that after learning how many groups are working on how many different priorities, they can change their minds if they wish.

2. Have each group report the priority it wants to work on. After all groups have reported, ask if any small group wants to select another priority.

3. Have each group spend 60 to 90 minutes working on the priority of its choice. It is all right for more than one group to work on any given priority. The goal right now is to be creative and to generate as many positive ideas as possible about how the school can improve in different areas. If some of the priorities are not selected, then it is not recommended that they be pursued in this setting. There is a reason for this, and the site team needs to research the reason why certain priorities were not selected for immediate discussion.

4. Have each group report out to the larger group a summary of the information it recorded on Worksheet 44 and ask the group to emphasize its ideas about what can be done immediately to better attain the vision in the group's selected area. Have each small group turn in its worksheet to the workshop facilitator for the site team to use in the future. Have each small group designate a contact person for the site team to contact for clarification and further information about the small group's contributions.

5. Indicate to the total group that the site team will create a listing of all the ideas for "things that can be done right now" and create a listing for everyone's use in the future. These ideas should be listed for each of the "priorities for improvement" that were worked on by the small groups. This listing can be an important resource for everyone in the school community as well as the site team.

6. End the session with a review of the next steps of the site team in the strategic planning process. That will be, of course, the development of program improvement plans for continuous school improvement in the priority areas identified by the group. Stress that the site team will continue to communicate the progress of its work and that the site team will request the continued support and participation of others in the future as it develops the program improvement plans. The public commitment to do so will again enhance the credibility of the site team and the trust that others will have in its future activities.

This concludes Phase 1 and Phase 2 of the strategic planning of the site team with the larger school community. The site team has now produced two of its required outputs—a shared vision of the future and priorities for program improvement. It has also created an important document that lists the things that can be done immediately to better meet the vision of the school.

Although the workshops with the school community are time consuming, they are critical to the future success of the site team.

1. The participation of the larger group gives credibility to the shared vision and the priorities for program improvement.

2. The diversity of perspectives and input from the workshop participants increases the quality of decision making by the site team.

3. The open and honest participation of the larger school community builds an atmosphere of shared commitment and responsibility.

WORKSHEET 44
Future Development Ideas (School Community Group Number ___)

Vision category: _____
(organizational climate, program plan, classroom interactions)

Vision area: _____

Step 1: Create a more detailed vision of this area.

1. What will it be like for the students, teachers, and parents?

2. What activities will they be involved in?

3. What is the nature of their interactions?

4. What outcomes (knowledge, skills, attitudes) will students and others gain as a result of this need being met?

Step 2: Collect information about the present.

1. What is it really like for the students, parents, and teachers?

2. What activities are they involved in?

3. What is the nature of their interactions?

4. What outcomes (knowledge, skills, attitudes) do they achieve now?

Step 3: Compare the present with the vision.

1. What is currently helpful in attaining the vision?

2. What is currently interfering with attaining the vision?

3. What can *you* do right now to better attain the vision?

4. What can others do right now to better attain the vision?

Larry J. Reynolds. *Successful Site-Based Management: A Practical Guide*, rev. ed. Copyright © 1997 by Corwin Press, Inc. Reprinted with permission.

Phase 3: Planning and Implementing Program Improvements

The site team can now focus on developing plans for program improvements. We believe that the problem-solving and decision-making sequence discussed in Chapter 9 will be a helpful approach to this ongoing task of the site team. And the strategic planning workshops with the school community should have provided the site team with a great deal of helpful information. Specifically, Worksheet 44 should identify potential causes of problems and solutions to consider in the problem-solving and decision-making sequence.

Before leaving this area, there are several suggestions for this process that may be helpful for the site team to consider.

1. As the site team reviews the priorities for program improvements, it is not necessary to work on them in order. In fact, we would suggest that the site team select one of the top priorities where the site team can use its current resources and have the greatest effect. If this priority requires a districtwide approach, significant changes in policy or levels of funding, and extensive training of staff, it may be better to immediately move to a different priority.

2. The site team will be wise to select one of the priorities where quick success can be demonstrated. This will be important for the site team itself, providing a sense of accomplishment. It will also provide quick and concrete evidence to the central office and the school community that the site team is working and working well.

3. The site team should also select an additional priority that is one of the tough problems. It may require more time and effort, but the site team must be willing to tackle the difficult issues as well.

4. In identifying solutions to selected priorities and problems, the site team should look for "little changes that have big effects." One of the areas in which this can occur is in the area of organizational climate, where a small increase in the amount of personal attention paid by teachers, parents, and students can have a large effect.

5. Consider priorities that address early the management and organizational climate needs of the school. These represent the real and immediate needs of teachers, students, and parents. As discussed earlier (see Chapter 7), when these issues are resolved to a satisfactory level, the overall instructional program and services will receive higher-quality attention.

6. When selecting priorities for program improvement, remember the special programs and projects that are currently under way as a result of earlier

district or school planning. It is important for the site team to understand the goals and strategies of these programs. Furthermore, the site team should ask those persons responsible for the special programs and projects to define how they relate to the overall shared vision of the future and the current priorities for school improvement. The site team will have to coordinate its own program improvement efforts with these programs to avoid competition among different groups and to be realistic about the remaining time and energy resources of the school for new program improvement efforts.

As the site team considers its program improvement plans, it should remember that the central office is now responsible for providing assistance to the individual schools in the development of those plans. The suggested restructuring of the central office to provide leadership and services to building site team was discussed in Chapter 5. The new roles of central office staff were based on the need to help schools answer the following seven questions:

1. What do you want to do?
2. What do you have to do?
3. What human resources do you need?
4. What program resources do you need?
5. What problems are you having?
6. What do you need to know?
7. What is the environment you require?

These seven questions may provide assistance to the site team in defining and communicating the assistance that would be helpful from the central office.

Evaluating School Improvement Efforts

It is critical for the site team to determine how to evaluate program improvement efforts prior to their adoption and implementation. The purpose here is not to specify all the different approaches that can be taken in program evaluations. We do believe, however, that the strategic planning model provides an important guide in evaluating whether the site team and program improvement efforts are focused on the right areas.

The "big questions" are sometimes the hardest to ask and the hardest to answer. However, that is the real function of the site team. Worksheet 45 provides another look at the strategic planning model and the questions that should be asked by the site team in its ongoing and continuous evaluation of the educational program and services of the school. Four questions provide a focus for the evaluation of the overall educational program of the school.

1. Is the vision of the future program and services of the school consistent with the external forces, student needs, and values and beliefs about education? This question is particularly critical today when schools are faced with rapid changes in our society, the communities we serve, and expectations for the programs and services we provide.

2. Is the day-to-day program of the school (organizational climate, program and staff organization, and classroom interactions) consistent with the vision of excellence? That is, are the actual experiences of students, parents, and staff consistent with the type of program and services we want to provide? All too frequently, our daily actions are inconsistent with our intentions, and we must have the courage and procedures to make the required adjustments.

3. Is the day-to-day program of the school providing the types and levels of student success that we desire? Frequently, when things are not working, we assume that success can be attained by trying the same thing again with increased effort. The current interest in restructuring is based on the assumption that we need to significantly alter how we view students and learning and how we organize our program and services if we are to increase levels of student success.

4. Are our definitions of success consistent with the future needs of our students in a rapidly changing and increasingly complex society? Student success may need to be defined more broadly, or differently, than it has been in the past.

WORKSHEET 45
Using the Strategic Planning Model for Continuous Evaluation

Is student success consistent with these criteria?

```
External forces ─┐                   ┌─ Organizational climate ─┐
                 │                   │                          │
Student needs ───┼── The vision ─────┼─ Program and             ├── Student success
                 │                   │  staff organization      │
Values and       │                   │                          │
beliefs ─────────┘                   └─ Classroom interactions ─┘
```

Are these consistent?   **Are these consistent?**   **Are these effective?**

Larry J. Reynolds. *Successful Site-Based Management: A Practical Guide*, rev. ed. Copyright © 1997 by Corwin Press, Inc. Reprinted with permission.

11

How Do We Know If We Are Making Progress?

Site-based management *is* a complex change. It requires significant changes at all levels of the organization and is likely to be disruptive of "the established order of things." Under site-based management, individuals need to alter their belief systems, acquire new knowledge, develop new skills, and alter previous patterns of behavior. These changes are all keyed to increasing the quality of decisions we make about educational programs and services, the "immediate" goal of site-based management. The ultimate success of site-based management will be judged by its effect on the success of students.

These relationships were diagrammed in Figure 2.1 on page 7.

In education, we frequently demand that new changes show an immediate and positive effect on students. We often "rush to judgment" by evaluating a new program before it has really been implemented. The new program may, at its early stages, exist more in name than it does in fact. Or its implementation may vary so widely from setting to setting that the new change cannot be expected to have a consistent effect across settings. Frequently, the effect on adults is immediate and is evident before the effect on educational programs and services and the success of students can be observed.

All too often we hear, "We tried that and it didn't work," when little effort was spent in trying to determine what would make the new program work. Time and again, it seems, the disruptive nature of new programs proves to be simply too demanding on the attention and energy of participants. New programs are often discontinued so we can return to the familiar ways of doing things, ways that have a higher comfort level.

Therefore, it makes sense to have the first step in the evaluation of site-based management determine whether it *is* being implemented and what it "looks like" in different schools in the district. It is likely that it will look very different in its implementation from one school to another.

The purpose of this final chapter is to recommend a number of strategies to monitor the efforts to implement site-based management across the district and to identify some of the problems that may be encountered. This information can then be used to assist different central office personnel, principals, and site teams in their implementation efforts. Specifically, the following areas will be addressed:

1. The role of the districtwide advisory group
2. Monitoring the process of implementing site-based management
3. Meeting the timelines
4. Monitoring site-team issues and decisions
5. Noticing the small changes, big effects
6. Questions to ask during the early stages
7. Questions to ask after implementation
8. Traditional concerns of the central office
9. Changing beliefs, values, and assumptions
10. The promise of site-based management

The Role of the Districtwide Advisory Group

When adopting site-based management, school districts often create a districtwide site team. The role of this group can vary greatly from district to district. In some settings, it has been formed to approve proposals from individual schools. Under this arrangement, the traditional pattern of control and compliance is likely to be continued. The only real change in the decision-making structure of the school district may be the substitution of a group for centralized decisions that were made earlier by an individual in the central office.

In other districts, the districtwide site team is made up of both central office and site-team representatives who serve in an advisory capacity. This approach can serve a number of useful functions during the early stages of implementing site-based management across the district. Some potential roles this group can play are the following:

1. Serving as a communication link across site teams
2. Identifying similar training needs across sites
3. Reviewing district parameters on what sites can do
4. Communicating with the board about site-based management, rather than individual sites
5. Assessing how the process of implementation is going

This advisory group may play a key role in the monitoring and evaluation of site-based management in the district.

Monitoring the Process of Implementation

The sequence of steps recommended for implementing site-based management can be used to monitor the progress of the district as a whole and of individual schools. If the sequence of steps is not followed, difficulties may arise. The following have been emphasized throughout our discussions:

1. The central office must do its work before the individual schools and site teams can be expected to do theirs.
2. The principal is the key to the success of site-based management. If the principal has not completed the steps necessary to facilitate the implementation of site-based management, the site team will not function effectively.
3. The site team should not be asked to make specific decisions before it has gone through the formation and training activities. To do so is to jeopardize the effectiveness of its leadership role and its internal decision-making process.
4. Different principals and schools will require different levels of support and different periods of time to complete the required sequence of steps.
5. The particular step currently in process by each individual principal and site team will affect the type of leadership and services required by the central office to support the implementation effort.

A checklist of the different steps is provided in Worksheet 46 as a means of monitoring the process of implementation across the district.

WORKSHEET 46
Monitoring the Process of Implementation

Steps in Implementing Site-Based Management	Completed			

Central office
1. Adopt a leadership perspective _____
2. Assess context of change _____
3. Adopt strategic planning model _____
4. Examine external forces _____
5. Examine student needs _____
6. Examine values and beliefs _____
7. Set overall district vision _____
8. Set expectations and parameters _____
9. Identify school's management needs _____
10. Create service and support roles _____

	School A	School B	School C	School D

Principal
11. Adopt systemwide perspective ___ ___ ___ ___
12. Assess context change ___ ___ ___ ___
13. Implement effectiveness plan ___ ___ ___ ___
14. Adopt leadership behaviors ___ ___ ___ ___
15. Define new roles and accountability ___ ___ ___ ___

Site team
16. Form the site team ___ ___ ___ ___
17. Learn new skills ___ ___ ___ ___
18. Adopt strategic planning model ___ ___ ___ ___
19. Examine external forces ___ ___ ___ ___
20. Examine student needs ___ ___ ___ ___
21. Examine values and beliefs ___ ___ ___ ___
22. Create a shared vision ___ ___ ___ ___
23. Assess current program ___ ___ ___ ___
24. Set priorities for improvement ___ ___ ___ ___
25. Plan, implement, and evaluate ___ ___ ___ ___

Larry J. Reynolds. *Successful Site-Based Management: A Practical Guide*, rev. ed. Copyright © 1997 by Corwin Press, Inc. Reprinted with permission.

Meeting the Timeline

The length of time needed to complete the 25 steps to implement site-based management will vary from district to district and from school to school within a given district. The factors that will influence the adoption of a realistic timeline for the overall district and individual schools may include the following:

1. The number and intensity of current issues in the district that will compete with site-based management for people's time and attention of district personnel (see Worksheet 6).

2. The number of special programs and projects in the district that will compete with site-based management for people's time and attention (see Worksheet 7).

3. The current level of leadership skills of central office personnel and building principals.

4. The current level of strategic planning skills and group process skills of central office personnel and building principals.

5. The current level of support and understanding of site-based management of key persons in the district's current decision-making structure (see Worksheet 4).

No matter what timeline is considered feasible, it is critical that an overall timeline be established for both the central office and the individual buildings. If this is not part of the expectations established for the change to site-based management, then it is not likely to occur. Site-based management will be given a lower priority than the immediate, short-term concerns of both the central office and individual buildings.

Different people will give different estimates on how long it takes to implement site-based management. Some believe 5 years is a reasonable estimate. It is believed, however, that the recommended process and sequence of steps can significantly reduce the time required for a successful change to site-based management. The timeline suggested for consideration is presented in Worksheet 47. Some districts and schools may be able to complete the necessary steps in less time, particularly if the required knowledge, attitudes, and skills already exist.

WORKSHEET 47
Suggested Timeline for Implementation

Steps in Implementing Site-Based Management	Year 1	Year 2	Year 3	Year 4	Year 5
Central office					
1. Adopt a leadership perspective	▓▓▓	___	___	___	___
2. Assess context of change	▓▓▓	___	___	___	___
3. Adopt strategic planning model	▓▓▓	___	___	___	___
4. Examine external forces	▓▓▓	___	___	___	___
5. Examine student needs	▓▓▓	___	___	___	___
6. Examine values and beliefs	▓▓▓	___	___	___	___
7. Set overall district vision	▓▓▓	___	___	___	___
8. Set expectations and parameters	▓▓▓	___	___	___	___
9. Identify school's management needs	▓▓▓	___	___	___	___
10. Create service and support roles	▓▓▓	___	___	___	___
Principal					
11. Adopt systemwide perspective	___	▓▓▓	___	___	___
12. Assess context change	___	▓▓▓	___	___	___
13. Implement effectiveness plan	___	▓▓▓	___	___	___
14. Adopt leadership behaviors	___	▓▓▓	___	___	___
15. Define new roles and accountability	___	▓▓▓	___	___	___
Site team					
16. Form the site team	___	▓▓▓	___	___	___
17. Learn new skills	___	▓▓▓	___	___	___
18. Adopt strategic planning model	___	___	▓▓▓	___	___
19. Examine external forces	___	___	▓▓▓	___	___
20. Examine student needs	___	___	▓▓▓	___	___
21. Examine values and beliefs	___	___	▓▓▓	___	___
22. Create a shared vision	___	___	▓▓▓	___	___
23. Assess current program	___	___	▓▓▓	___	___
24. Set priorities for improvement	___	___	▓▓▓	___	___
25. Plan, implement, and evaluate	___	___	___	▓▓▓	▓▓▓

NOTE: Shaded areas are the recommended times.

Larry J. Reynolds. *Successful Site-Based Management: A Practical Guide*, rev. ed. Copyright © 1997 by Corwin Press, Inc. Reprinted with permission.

Monitoring Site-Team Issues and Decisions

It may also be helpful to monitor the types of issues and decisions that are considered by the site teams in each individual school. The potential effect of site-based management on student success is dependent on the site team's focusing its energy on school improvement plans that emerge from the strategic planning process. Instead, however, the site team may spend its time reacting to immediate events and issues of the school.

If this is the case, the discussion of organizational effectiveness in Chapter 7 can be helpful. The issues and decisions of the site team may very well reflect the level of the school's organizational effectiveness. The five steps to organizational effectiveness are as follows:

1. Meeting the management needs of the school
2. Creating a positive organizational climate
3. Developing positive attitudes and beliefs about change
4. Developing a schoolwide perspective of the educational program
5. Adopting the strategic planning model for school improvement

The time and energy spent on each category will give the central office an indication of the assistance each school needs to move to the next level of effectiveness. A sample checklist is provided in Worksheet 48.

WORKSHEET 48
Checklist of Site-Team Issues and Decisions: School A

Type of Issues and Decisions	No. of Decisions	Amount of Time
Meeting the management needs of the school	_____	_____
Creating a positive organizational climate	_____	_____
Developing positive attitudes and beliefs about change	_____	_____
Developing a schoolwide perspective of the educational program	_____	_____
Using the strategic planning model and school improvement plans	_____	_____

Larry J. Reynolds. *Successful Site-Based Management: A Practical Guide*, rev. ed. Copyright © 1997 by Corwin Press, Inc. Reprinted with permission.

Another simple observation about issues and decisions may be helpful. The district's expectations for decision making can be used as a checklist to see if the site teams are making the kinds of decisions that are likely to affect student success (see Worksheet 14). The checklist will also reveal the patterns that exist across the district and those schools that have a significantly different pattern of decision making. (It should be remembered that the differences among schools may be due to their differing needs.)

Worksheet 14 can be modified and used by the site teams and central office for this monitoring activity. This revision is presented as Worksheet 49.

WORKSHEET 49
Checklist of Decision Making in Different Schools

Decision Areas (check those that apply)	Actual Involvement in			
	School A	School B	School C	School D
Distribution of budget for staff positions	___	___	___	___
Distribution of budget for supplies and materials	___	___	___	___
Identification of student and program needs	___	___	___	___
Identification of goals and directions for the school improvement efforts	___	___	___	___
Identification of learner outcomes for students	___	___	___	___
Identification of the curriculum and the needed instructional strategies	___	___	___	___
Identification of policies and procedures, for example, discipline, attendance, homework	___	___	___	___
Identification of performance indicators of student learning and success	___	___	___	___
Distribution of staff development moneys	___	___	___	___
Selection of new staff members	___	___	___	___
Participation in staff evaluation	___	___	___	___
Identification of priorities for building maintenance and improvement	___	___	___	___

Larry J. Reynolds. *Successful Site-Based Management: A Practical Guide*, rev. ed. Copyright © 1997 by Corwin Press, Inc. Reprinted with permission.

Noticing the Small Changes, Big Effects

It is important to remember that school improvements in all areas—organizational climate, program organization, and classroom interaction—can be attained by the cumulative effect of numerous small changes. Whereas significant changes in the structure of the budget, program, and staff of a school may be highly visible and easily attributed to site-based management, small changes can often be more easily and immediately implemented. Furthermore, these small changes and the immediate success that they bring may well help build the positive energy needed to move to the point where larger and more complex changes can be considered and planned.

When the school community is assessing the current program and identifying actions that can be taken immediately, the opportunity exists for identifying small changes with big effects. The central office also has this opportunity because of its new roles of leadership and service. Examples of these small changes might include the following:

1. Changing the scheduling of classes so that teachers work with the same students more often
2. Having high school science teachers spend a semester working with elementary teachers to help them maintain and build students' interest in science
3. Creating a way to provide teachers with information about their students' learning styles
4. Increasing the informal interaction of teachers across grade-level and subject area boundaries
5. Arranging for peer tutoring during study halls
6. Inviting the state's "teacher of the year" to demonstrate "five ways to capture students' interest" to the district's new teachers
7. Recognizing those district staff members who have found their own "small changes, big effects"

It may well be that the small changes in the district are the best indicator of attaining the goal of the leadership efforts of the central office, principals, and site teams: to allow schools and individual teachers to express their creativity in developing strategies at the school level for program improvement.

Questions to Ask During the Early Stages

Site-based management is a complex change that can be expected to attain a wide range of benefits to the district. During the early stages of implementation, the increased involvement in decision making by the site team and the school community may have a number of positive effects. Changes may well be occurring that are likely to increase the quality of decisions about the educational program and, ultimately, the success of students. It will be important to identify and communicate these early benefits to members of the school community to reinforce the implementation effort.

The actual effect of site-based management on the schools can be determined by reexamining the list of expectations of the potential benefits of site-based management (see Worksheet 13). After the individual schools have completed their shared vision and begun to implement program improvement plans, this early listing can be examined again to determine how well those early expectations are being realized.

The actual effect of site-based management can be compared to early expectations for the district as a whole, and differences among buildings can be identified. This review also provides an opportunity to solicit comments about other effects and benefits of site-based management. It may well be that there have been additional positive effects of site-based management that were not expected prior to beginning its implementation.

Worksheet 13 can be modified and given to central office staff, principals, site teams, and the school community. This revision is provided as Worksheet 50.

WORKSHEET 50
Actual Benefits of Site-Based Management

Potential Benefits	Actual Effect			
	(low) 1	2	3	4 (high)
Greater principal awareness of issues and concerns	___	___	___	___
Greater staff awareness of issues and concerns	___	___	___	___
Greater staff awareness of student needs	___	___	___	___
More effective response to student needs	___	___	___	___
More innovation and change	___	___	___	___
More staff involvement in decision making	___	___	___	___
Better communication among staff	___	___	___	___
Greater staff cohesiveness	___	___	___	___
More ownership and commitment of program by staff	___	___	___	___
Increased staff awareness of effective programs	___	___	___	___
Improved attainment of student outcomes	___	___	___	___
More parent involvement in decision making	___	___	___	___
Increased support from parents	___	___	___	___

Larry J. Reynolds. *Successful Site-Based Management: A Practical Guide,* rev. ed. Copyright © 1997 by Corwin Press, Inc. Reprinted with permission.

Questions to Ask After Implementation

As site-based management becomes established in the district and in individual schools, it is then possible to assess whether site-based management is beginning to have the desired effect. Rather than asking questions that will help in the implementation of site-based management, the central office, districtwide advisory groups, principals, and site teams may wish to ask questions about the effectiveness of site-based management. These questions would be premature to ask during the early stages of implementation but are appropriate once site-based management exists in fact. Questions such as those shown in Table 11.1 are suggested.

Traditional Concerns of the Central Office

One of the frequent patterns of site-based management is that it fails because it becomes "too successful." Site teams may "take the ball and run," spending considerable time and energy to develop a new program or altered budget allocations only to find them vetoed by the central office. This is one of the reasons why it has been stressed that the central office must specify its expectations and parameters of the decision-making authority of the site teams in the beginning. However, it is doubtful that all the potential issues between the site teams and the central office can be anticipated in advance.

The central office needs to understand that despite its proclamations in support of decentralized decision making, its "moment of truth" is going to come. Because site-based management takes time to develop, the old system of control and compliance may not be challenged for some time. While site teams are forming and undergoing training, the risk levels for the central office may not be high. After all, no one has really decided anything different, yet. If the central office perceives a significant decrease in its control over the school and an increase in the risk of a decision, it is likely to respond in the traditional manner. The critical point comes when the risk is perceived as greater than the control of the central office (see Figure 11.1).

The central office must recognize when its change to a leadership role will require real risk taking on its part. If this situation is analyzed for what it is, then the central office can be honest about its response to initiatives by individual schools that represent significant departures from previous programs, policies, or practices.

It is unlikely that the site team will anticipate all of the questions or concerns of the central office as the team prepares its school improvement plans. If the central office can identify its concerns and adopt a problem-solving perspective, it may be that the site team's proposed change can be satisfactorily clarified or even modified.

TABLE 11.1 Questions to Ask After Implementation

About principals and site teams	1. Is the site team dealing with significant issues? 2. Is the team effective as a decision-making group? 3. Is there a collaborative relationship between the principal and the site team? 4. How is the site team perceived by other members of the organization?
About individual schools	1. Does everyone understand the shared vision of the future? 2. Does everyone understand his or her role and contribution in attaining the vision? 3. Does the vision guide daily action by individuals? 4. Is there a commitment and concerted effort to implement school improvement plans?
About the districtwide effort	1. Are the early expectations for site-based management being attained? 2. Do the schools request and receive support and assistance from the central office staff? 3. Is there increased flexibility and variability among individual school programs? 4. Are school programs perceived as more effective?
About students	1. Are there real student benefits from school improvement decisions and site-based management in terms of student success?

However, rejecting the proposal without an effort by the central office to preserve the integrity of site-based management will seriously erode the credibility and trust of the central office with regard to site-based management.

Changing Beliefs, Values, and Assumptions

Site-based management is a vehicle for the restructuring of our schools that requires a significant departure from our traditional beliefs about education and about how schools should be run. Our traditional system is based on a centralized system where decisions are made by a few at the top of the organizational structure, an assumption that standardization is necessary to assure quality, a belief that the process of education can be broken down into independent subject areas and

How Do We Know If We Are Making Progress?

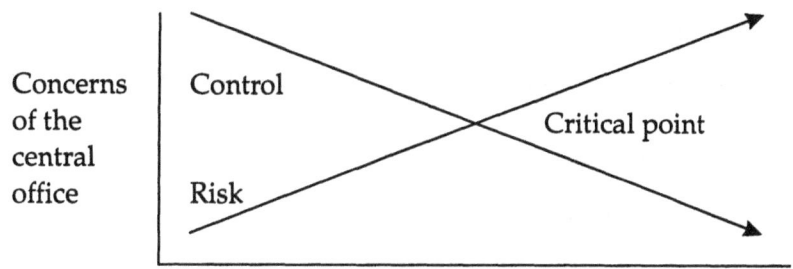

Figure 11.1. Traditional Concerns of the Central Office

support services that require increasing levels of specialization, a perception that the needs of the community and its students are constant over time, and a controlling of the relationships among participants of the organization by clearly defined policies and procedures.

Our traditional system has served us well in the past. But, as our communities have become less stable, as the needs and characteristics of our parents and students population have shifted, and as our society has changed, our schools have remained much the same. We have focused our efforts to improve education by trying to increase the efficiency and effectiveness of an existing structure that is no longer suited to the task at hand. To redesign our schools to meet the changing realities, a significant restructuring of our beliefs, values, and assumptions is required.

The Promise of Site-Based Management

Site-based management is one of the key strategies to create a new organizational structure for schools that encourages the flexibility, initiative, and innovation we need to keep pace with the changes around us. In contrast to the traditional structure of schools, site-based management encourages those closest to the school's clients and customers (the students and parents) to make key decisions, promotes variety and flexibility in educational programs as a means to excellence, requires coordination and integration across subject areas and a schoolwide perspective, recognizes that the needs of the community and students change over time, and creates relationships that are based on a commitment to common goals.

As emphasized throughout this book, for this new structure to emerge, significant changes must be made in how we think about the administration of our schools.

We must also devote our administrative energies to creating the organizational components that will support the success of site-based management:

1. Adopting a systemwide perspective
2. Understanding the context of change
3. Developing leadership perspectives and skills
4. Creating a shared vision
5. Developing strategic planning skills
6. Defining new roles
7. Enhancing the work environment
8. Understanding group dynamics
9. Clarifying accountability

These nine components indicate the new perspectives and skills necessary for the central office, principals, and site-team members to transform our schools. These perspectives and skills are built into the 25 steps (and supporting worksheets) proposed for implementing effective site-based management. This book is, therefore, a practical guide that describes *how* to implement effective site-based management. School renewal efforts often fail, not because people are insincere but because such significant, systemwide change is difficult and unfamiliar. By adopting these nine perspectives and following the 25 steps, the "how" is no longer a concern. Instead, change efforts can be begun with confidence and optimism, and the promise of site-based management can be realized.

References

Bennis, W., & Nanus, B. (1985). *Leaders.* New York: Harper & Row.

Fiske, E. B. (1991). *Smart schools, smart kids: Why do some schools work?* New York: Simon & Schuster.

Glickman, C. D. (1993). *Renewing America's schools: A guide for school-based action.* San Francisco: Jossey-Bass.

Kotter, J. P. (1990). What leaders really do. *Harvard Business Review, 90*(3), 103-111.

Kouzes, J. M., & Posner, B. Z. (1987). *The leadership challenge: How to get extraordinary things done in organizations.* San Francisco: Jossey-Bass.

Mauriel, J. J. (1989). *Strategic leadership for schools: Creating and sustaining productive change.* San Francisco: Jossey-Bass.

Murphy, J., & Beck, L. G. (1995). *School-based reform: Taking stock.* Thousand Oaks, CA: Corwin.

Robbins, S. P. (1993). *Organizational behavior: Concepts, controversies and applications.* Englewood Cliffs, NJ: Prentice Hall.

Smith, H. (1995). *Rethinking America: Innovative strategies and partnerships in business and education.* New York: Avon.

The Corwin Press logo—a raven striding across an open book—represents the happy union of courage and learning. We are a professional-level publisher of books and journals for K–12 educators, and we are committed to creating and providing resources that embody these qualities. Corwin's motto is "Success for All Learners."

In compliance with GPSR, should you have any concerns about the safety of this product, please advise: International Associates Auditing & Certification Limited The Black Church, St Mary's Place, Dublin 7, D07 P4AX Ireland EUAR@ie.ia-net.com

www.ingramcontent.com/pod-product-compliance
Lightning Source LLC
Chambersburg PA
CBHW081420300426
44110CB00016BA/2328